I0828245

Significant Journey

The story of a
prodigal daughter's
wanderings from the
mountains of Afghanistan
to the wilderness of Canada

Judy de Chantal

TEACH Services, Inc.
www.TEACHServices.com

This book was written to provide truthful information in regard to the subject matter covered. The author assumes full responsibility for the accuracy of all facts and quotations as cited in this book. The opinions expressed in this book are the author's personal views and interpretation of the Bible, Spirit of Prophecy, and/or contemporary authors and do not necessarily reflect those of TEACH Services, Inc.

This book is sold with the understanding that the publisher is not engaged in giving spiritual, legal, medical, or other professional advice. If authoritative advice is needed, the reader should seek the counsel of a competent professional

---

ISBN-13: 978-1-57258-661-1 (Paperback)
ISBN-13: 978-1-57258-662-8 (Hardback)
ISBN-13: 978-1-57258-663-51 (Ebook)
Library of Congress Control Number: 2011926387

Published by
TEACH Services, Inc.
www.TEACHServices.com

Dedicated with love to Alain,
the French Canadian to whom I gave a lift to Athens.
He has been with me ever since,
and I am glad we will be together for eternity.

And our children—
Jacinthe and Ryan, Jonquille and Josh—
who inspired me to tell this story.

"That guy was shooting at us!" I cried. Just then I heard a second shot.

Alain slammed on the brakes. In an instant we were surrounded by Turkish soldiers jumping out of jeeps and yanking us out of our old Volkswagen van. I was in stocking feet in the ice and mud. The uniformed men were tearing through our belongings, tossing our things onto the snow bank on the side of the road.

I in English and Alain in French were asking, "What is going on? What do you want?"

But our questions were ignored. Desperate, with tears in my eyes, above the confusion and chaos, I yelled one last question, "Does anyone speak English?"

Suddenly behind me I heard, "Hello, how are you?"

Whirling around, I found a young soldier, smiling broadly. Frantically, I grasped him by the sleeve.

"Oh thank goodness you speak English! Please tell us what is happening? What do they want? What is going on?"

"Today the sun is shining!" He smiled a pleased smile, and my heart fell to the bottom of my frozen feet. Turning away to hide my tears, in dismay I heard him repeat, "Hello, how are you?" Alain was as white as a sheet. We didn't need a weather report to tell us that no sun would be shining on us today.

Part One

On the Road

"O, Lord, you have searched my heart and
know me inside and out.
You know my comings and goings and
discern my thoughts before I think them.
You walk beside me all day long,
And when I lie down at night, you're still there.
You know everything I do and say.
There's not a word that comes from my mouth,
O Lord, that you don't know beforehand.
You are behind me, in front of me and
all around me wherever I go.
You have touched me and drawn me close to you.
I can't comprehend it.
It's so wonderful that no matter how hard I try to understand,
I can't grasp it all."
Psalms 139:1-6

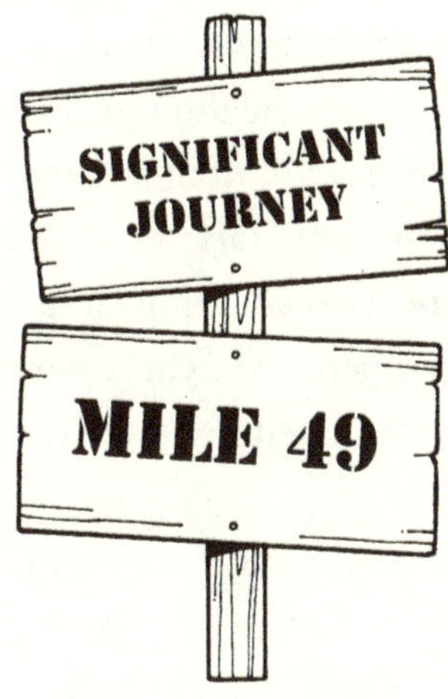

It was a muggy August night seven months earlier when I dragged my fifty-pound backpack into a better position so that I could grab my skis off the baggage claim belt. Lugging them into the Frankfurt, Germany, train station, the exhilaration of this first big solo trip masked the fatigue of my eleven-hour flight.

"American?" A stout trim-mustached gentleman inquired in a heavy German accent.

My American flag patch sat new and cleanly stitched on the pocket of my jeans. "Yes, from Washington."

"Oh yes, Washington D.C.!"

And for the next year, I would be replying, "Well, no, the Washington on the Pacific Ocean, near Seattle."

I decided to travel to Europe in the summer of 1972 after becoming friends with some skiers in British Columbia, Canada. A handful of them were Canadians, but most were from European countries. All of them had jobs around Vancouver.

One of these friends, Ilana, was going to Germany to visit relatives, and she encouraged me to come. Our plan was to travel around for the summer and then work at a ski resort for the winter. I asked for and was granted a year leave of absence from my job as a school nurse.

Armed with a copy of the travel book *Europe on Five Dollars a Day*, traveler's checks to carry me through a year, with some extra for a car, I bought a round-trip ticket from Vancouver to Frankfurt.

I found renters for my little farm on Puget Sound who wanted a furnished house and agreed to care for my dog, cat, and horse. Packing my car to the ceiling with personal items I would store with friends in Vancouver, I headed north. I tied my travel backpack and skis to the car roof.

But first I stopped to say good-bye to my parents.

"We got you this for your trip," my mom said as she handed me a small wrapped gift. I thanked them both and kissed them good-bye. Daddy gave me a final bear hug. As I hurried to the car, I turned and waved. They stood together in the doorway of their little cottage throwing kisses until I drove out of sight.

I didn't open the package until I stopped to buy a sandwich. It was a little travel Bible. Inside the front cover, in my mom's distinctive handwriting, she had written, "We will be praying that God will keep you safe on this journey and guide you back home soon." Under their signatures were a dozen X's and O's.

". . . and guide you back home soon . . ." I knew that phrase had a deeper meaning for my parents. My family were Christians. I grew up attending church every weekend, and I went to Christian schools. I believed in God. I always had and was confident I always would. I didn't have unpleasant feelings toward Christians or religion, and I didn't have doubts about the Bible being true. But I didn't profess to be a Christian. In my mind, my stance was simple enough. I would have to bring my life into alignment with my beliefs and that seemed overwhelming. I had too much to do and was too busy for that right now.

In late afternoon, I arrived at the Canadian border.

"Where are you going with all of this stuff?' the uniformed guard gruffly asked as he stepped out of his booth.

"To Vancouver. I am going on a trip to Europe, and friends are storing these things for me," I answered with a smile.

"You can't bring your things into this country if you aren't a citizen!"

"But all I want to do is store them for a year." I caught my breath.

"Sorry."

"I don't know what to do! My plane leaves tonight," I responded, dismayed.

"Pull in over there and go see what the immigration officer says."

Minutes later, armed with a pink slip, I was a landed immigrant in Canada, and I was headed north again! My New Zealand and British friends were upset to find out that I, an American, was able to immigrate in ten minutes while they, although part of the British Commonwealth, spent eight months getting their papers.

Thus began a journey to faraway places and then into the wilderness, a journey that changed my life.

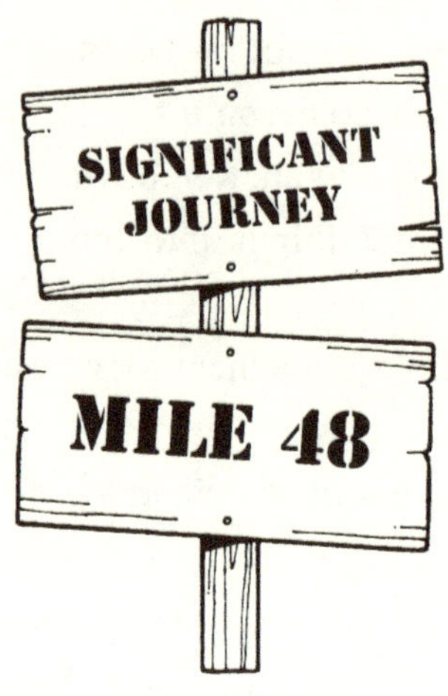

A five-hundred-dollar car was hard to find, at least one that ran, and one we could sleep in. But that was all I could spend. Such a car was really hard to find because I was in Germany and I did not speak the language. It was even more difficult to find because I was in a tiny Rhine River village far from car lots, staying with the aunt and uncle of my friend, Ilana, and they thought it was a very foolish idea—the idea of two girls from North America traveling and camping in a car all over Europe for months and months. They were probably right.

Her uncle kept sending people to talk us out of the trip or to offer more sensible automobiles. Perhaps a nice sedan or a solid little compact, they proposed, but we could not afford any of them. We had been looking for two weeks, and I had begun to wonder if we would have to hitchhike. That idea would have really distressed Ilana's aunt and uncle, let alone our parents!

Then one afternoon a beat-up blue and white 1958 Volkswagen van was brought for us to see. Except for the bench seats, it was stripped to the metal inside. No extras, not even a speedometer that worked, but it started with the third crank of the key, and it was only two hundred and eighty dollars. It was perfect.

Miles of red tape and four days later, we headed south, excited to be on our way, and enjoying each kilometer. Hastily hemmed red-checked gingham curtains hung in our windows. A sheet of plywood balanced on the folded-up backseat and held our skis, sleeping bags, and a candle in a holder. A red plastic water jug was propped on the floor between our packs. Stars and maple leaves cut out of red contact paper adorned our van's exterior and announced the American and Canadian inside. We named the van the "Belly Button Bomb" in honor of the big round VW emblem on its chubby front.

Two young girls in the elderly van puttered into Munich, Germany. Making our fun footloose way south, our travel plans were structured mostly around what famous activities were taking place in Europe and the home addresses given to us by our European ski friends back in Canada.

The 1972 Summer Olympics in Munich were in full swing. We arrived just days after the bombing by terrorists of the Israeli's compound. The flowers woven into the fencing spoke of the tragedy. It was a sober beginning of a year on the road. Ilana was born in Israel. Her parents, both born in Germany, lost their families in the Holocaust, so this horrible incident was very upsetting. Ilana's cousin who we were visiting in Munich and whose wife made the best noodle soup ever had a tattooed forearm testifying to ten years spent in a Nazi labor camp. He was twenty-five when he was freed. Ilana and I camped next to a cathedral in front of their apartment. It felt safe under the hourly chiming of the church bells, but one night someone tried to open our side doors. Thankfully, when we shouted they ran away.

Our side doors didn't slide open like the newer models. They swung outwards and only locked with a key from the outside. To lock ourselves in, we pried a stout piece of plank between the two door handles and the door. One day I was inside alone, so I slipped the small plank in place. Ilana returned and from the outside turned the handle, and it passed neatly under the piece of plank and the door opened! We were appalled, thinking about all the nights we had slept in an unlocked van believing we were secure! We then added a rope and tied the handles shut with a lot of knots to crank up our level of security.

The Olympics were ending soon, so it was time for us to move on. Several of our friends who were part of our Canadian ski group were now back home in Switzerland. We dined on Raclette and fondue, watched the cow parades from the mountains to winter pastures, their huge brass bells clanging, and shopped in Geneva and Zurich with our friends. Our plan was to work at a ski area for the winter, so we applied for jobs in Davos, a famous resort in Switzerland, giving Athens, Greece, as our contact address. We planned to reach there by October.

Youth hostels offered cheap rooms and were scattered all throughout Europe. We marked the map with their locations, which helped us plan a route for our travels. But there were downsides to staying at these hostels, the main one being that most featured only crowded and noisy dorm rooms as accommodations. If we parked in their parking lots, we could use the showers, wash our clothes in their sinks, and write letters under their electric lights, all the while enjoying the safety within their gates, but sleep in the peace and quiet of our van. We convinced ourselves we were not taking advantage of the system since we were not using their beds. We managed to pass unnoticed amidst the crowds of travelers . . . until Genoa.

It was 5:30 in the morning. Harsh pounding on our van door and a shrill Italian voice woke us up out of a deep sleep. A short burley man, some sort of youth hostel official, was demanding payment or we were to leave immediately. It was obvious we had been found out.

On a five-dollar-a-day budget (we believed the book and proved it workable), we had no spare change, so we started the car, shifted into low gear, and moved toward the closed gate. Our gatekeeper jogged alongside us, voice in high gear, arms flailing, in quite a dither. We figured it was best to move on out of his way as fast as possible.

But there was a problem. He wanted us to pay *and* to leave, and judging by the knife he had pulled out of his pocket and the gestures toward our tires, he planned to make sure we paid OR we couldn't leave!

But wait! The early morning bakery truck was ringing at the gate; the gate we would exit, and the driver was ringing to enter. Our gatekeeper was in a quandary. The baker impatiently wanted in. We anxiously wanted out. We saved the distressed gate guy the trouble of making a decision as we slipped like an eel through the opening gate, leaving our burly bellower behind with the baked goods.

Literally, we had been saved by the bell.

It was a September evening in Budapest. Balmy, the night air sparkled with lights across the Danube River. Three flights up in a city apartment a small stout woman answered to our ring. Ilana spoke German and used her German-Hungarian dictionary to explain that we were friends of the son of a cousin of this lady of the house. None of the three of us had met, let alone been acquainted with this cousin, this connection, this name in our address book. So we were certainly an unexpected surprise on her doorstep. Graciously she took us in, literally off the street, fed us, and showed us her city. For two days, we were her guests.

Unashamedly, we made our way across Europe—Hungary, Lichtenstein, Luxembourg, Germany, Switzerland, Austria, France, and Czechoslovakia—with this little book filled with the names of relatives of friends back home. They proved to be gracious hosts. We ate at their tables, enjoyed their company, and got acquainted with Europe from the inside out. I was grateful that Ilana could speak several languages. I spent my time smiling and nodding, accompanied by my mantra, "What did he/she say?"

One day while we were ambling along on the country roads

in Hungary, I happened to mention the word "Sabbath" in our conversation.

"Do you mean Saturday?" Ilana asked.

"Yes, Saturday is the Sabbath in the denomination I grew up in," I answered. "Your family is Jewish, right?"

Ilana was surprised at all the commonalities of the religions of our youth. She told me of the various religious holidays that were still a tradition in her family, and I spoke of those elements of mine that matched hers. I felt a twinge of guilt because I couldn't bring myself to speak of believing in God to her. But it passed. It was best to keep my mind on how well my life was going.

The two of us had a lot in common, and she was a good traveling companion. We both liked to read, hike, ski, and meet new people.

In Rome, we were in line to see the Sistine Chapel when we struck up a conversation with two American guys behind us. I asked what they did for a living. They said they worked for the biggest business in the world.

"IBM?" I guessed.

"No. . ."

"Ford Company?"

"No. . ." They were both smiling by then.

After a few more wrong guesses, desperately I blurted out, "The Mafia?"

"No. . ."

They were Roman Catholic priests.

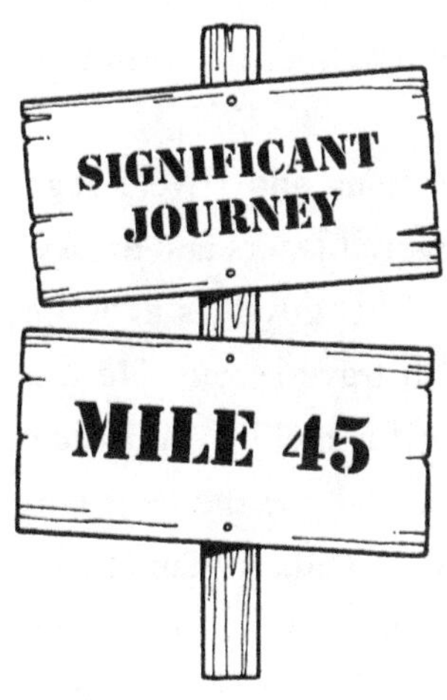

It was the end of October. The Rome youth hostel was on the grounds of the 1954 Olympic village. Other vans camped, like us, in the parking lot. It was 1972 and the apex of backpack travelers on the road in Europe. A kid from New Jersey with a van parked beside us had posted a sign in the hostel asking for riders to share expenses to Athens. He had too many responses, so he asked us if we would be interested in taking some paying passengers to Athens. That was where we are heading too, right?

It was a nice idea. Gas was expensive in Italy. "Send some of them over, and we will decide," I told him.

That evening as I was picking my way down the staircase, clean hair dripping, towel folded around clothes scrubbed in the second floor sink of the hostel, concentrating on making a nonchalant exit past the check-in clerk to my van, I was tapped on the shoulder. I turned to find this bearded, dark-haired guy looking down at me.

"You are heading to Athens in Greece?" he inquired in a soft voice.

"Well . . . yes." I was curious how he knew that but more curious about his accent. Was it French?

"A guy in a van said for me to find you here. Would you give me a ride?" He brushed a curly strand of hair out of his brown eyes. Our New Jersey parking lot neighbor had sent him to inquire about a ride to Athens.

I paused, not sure. Ilana and I were regular people, she a bank teller, me a nurse. We wore blazers and dressy shoes, sometimes even dresses as we traveled. This guy was a "hippie," had very long hair, and wore big boots with frayed jeans. He was nice looking, but that wasn't a good criterion for picking up a rider. Would this be a safe thing to do? Well, we could use the help with the gas expenses. He seemed OK, but I needed to talk to Ilana first.

"I will talk to my friend. Why don't you come to the van in an hour for our answer, OK? It is the blue and white one with the red stars and maple leaves."

Two days later he was heading to south Italy with us along with a Pennsylvanian, another paying passenger sent from the New Jersey van. The curly headed one was Alain. He had been on the road for four months, stopping to work when he ran out of funds. He had just come from working in the grape harvest in southern France. His home was in a small French village in Quebec, Canada.

It was early in the morning when we stopped at Pompeii, and I was jolted by what I saw. This once prosperous city had been caught completely by surprise by the eruption of the overlooking volcano, Mount Vesuvius. The shapes of people were seen clutching their treasures, frozen in flight by the enveloping molten lava. Roadways, rooms, and rampart remains were still standing. But all the people had perished. Wild columbine pushed up between cobblestones. Dates dangled from trees. A translucent aqua sky shimmered above, probably just as on that morning long ago.

A Bible verse from school popped into my head, "While people are saying, 'Peace and safety,' destruction will come on them suddenly . . . but you . . . are not in darkness so that this day should surprise you"

(1 Thess. 5:3, 4, NIV).

"But you are not in darkness . . ." This phrase replayed in my mind for the rest of the day. It was true. I knew all about the Bible. I should be in good shape, right?

Into the late afternoon, we meandered across the ankle of Italy. We were headed to Brindisi in the heel of Italy to cross by ferry to Greece. The warm, early fall countryside was peaceful. Crickets chirped. Farmers cleared their fields. Cattle chewed their cud in yellow pastures. The road was lazy and curvy, and we did not drive fast. The van was running well. We were becoming experts on figuring out its idiosyncrasies. For one thing, something to do with the "brushes" in the ignition caused it to remain silent with the first turn or two of the key. No sound at all, but no problem, after the third or fourth crank, the ignition would fire up the engine and we would be on our way.

For another thing, we didn't have a gas gauge, but someone somewhere along the way, told us that Volkswagen vans in this age bracket and caliber had gas tanks that would hold enough gas to drive a little more than 200 miles. So we kept a small notebook taped to the dash with a pencil tied on a string, and whenever the mileage showed close to 200 miles, we filled the tank. On a sandy stretch of road, we coasted to a stop. We had forgotten to check our notebook, and the gas tank was dry.

It was already dusk so we decided to camp. Except for the Pennsylvanian, who had some sort of time schedule, the rest of us had no appointments for the next year, so were not in any rush. But a policeman came along with other ideas about where we should park. Understanding our situation, he took Alain to a station to get a tank of gas, but it was closed. We would have to wait until morning, so the policeman helped push us a bit further onto the shoulder.

The next day in Brindisi, the village with the ferry docks, it took at least two hours to get tickets and papers cleared for the van to travel on to Greece later that night. After a dinner of bread, cheese, and apples, Alain and I found ourselves strolling together through the streets. Not only did he speak in a soft voice, but he had a nice quiet way about him. He was the middle of five children—an older sister and three brothers. He had been hitchhiking through Europe, traveling alone and sleeping in his pup tent in city parks and along roadsides. In Spain he was dragged into the police station for setting up his tent in a city park. The officers began to harass him, but when there was a lull, he dodged through an open door and escaped. No one followed him, but he left behind some of his camping equipment. He took passage on a ship from Genoa to Rome where we met him.

We passed a small chapel with tiny stained glass windows, and I peered in the door. It was so small that I could see the expression on the face of the statue of Mary up front. She had clear plastic tears slipping down her rosy cheeks. An elderly woman dressed in black was quietly sobbing out her prayers as she knelt at the painted feet. It made me sad, and I couldn't stop thinking about that upturned kerchiefed face all evening.

I don't mention my ties to Christianity to Alain. Since I was not living the lifestyle, I didn't want to misrepresent God or be a hypocrite. Wouldn't God appreciate me protecting His name by this decision? Or would there be tears to His eyes right now? Real, not plastic ones. Later when I had time, I planned to think about that more.

Early the next morning our van pulled into Greece after the long overnight ferry trip across the sea. Winding around the mountains and chugging up the inclines, we took turns reading the maps and driving. On one curve a flock of sheep swarmed around us. Little stone cottages hid in the folds of the hills.

By now, the drive itself was the most enjoyable part for me, not the destination. Alain and I found ourselves spending more and more time talking alone, talking about our travels so far, about where we wanted to go, and about each other. He was comfortable to be around. I felt as if I had known him much longer, and I could tell that Alain did not want this trip to Athens to end.

Testing the Pennsylvanian's patience to the limit, we dilly-dallied along, enjoying the sites, dragging out the drive to Athens into several days. We pacified him with the fact that driving slower saved fuel, for which he was helping to pay.

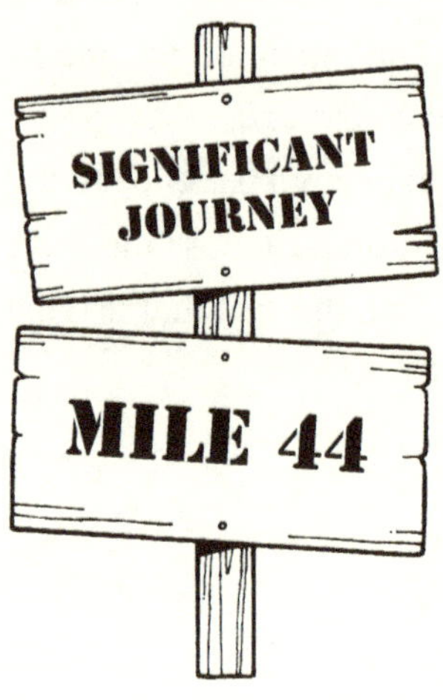

The Pennsylvanian headed off to Yugoslavia before the dust settled on the curb in Athens. Ilana, Alain, and I found good souflakis to eat before dropping by the American Express office to check for mail. We then headed to the Canadian Embassy to read the newspapers and later found a great place to camp in the middle of Athens on a hill called Lykavittos.

All to soon it was time to take my friend, Ilana, to the airport and say good-bye. She had received a letter telling her that she had a job in Davos, Switzerland, for the winter ski season. Unfortunately, my work application had been turned down. First she would fly to Israel, her place of birth, for a short visit. We planned to connect back up in the spring in central Europe. We stood at the airport waving until we saw her dark braids disappear as she boarded the plane.

Alain and I sat in the airport parking lot for awhile after she left. Not only did we need some time to decide what we would do next, but we also had forty-five minutes paid for in the parking meter.

So, for that moment, building a cupboard from a recycled wood box was our goal. Alain fastened it to the back of the front seat then added some shelves. The two pans and teapot now had a place of their own. Some narrow strips shaped with his hatchet and nailed to the front edge kept things from falling out. He sanded the top smooth so that we could use it for a table. Melted candle wax rubbed into the surface would make it easier to clean. A second box fitted beside it would serve as a place for the cookstove.

Alain had taken charge of the van's maintenance and my safety. And I was more than happy about it. There was no question by now that we would travel together. We had so many countries more to see—we might even go all the way to India and Nepal.

We wandered around Athens, watching people bargain in the markets and sitting in the sunset under the Acropolis. I told him about my folks, my brother and sister, my work and my animals back home. He was easy to talk with, a good listener. We never seemed to run out of things to talk about or to do. Just sitting on a step somewhere watching the people was a great pastime with him.

Early one morning Alain woke to a hand groping through the tiny round window of his tent just above his head. The thief left in a rush when Alain grabbed his wrist and gave it a wrench. We moved and set up another camp area on a grassy open spot on top of a mountain. But the next morning we woke up in the middle of a soccer game. The players kicked the ball around us as if we were invisible.

Then, roaming the streets one day, we forgot where we had parked the van, and we spent an hour helplessly looking for our vehicle. Methodically we walked up and down each street until at last we found it. The city had begun to wear on us. It was time to get out of Athens. Later that day we bought one-way third-class tickets on the next boat to the Greek island of Crete.

On the overnight ferry ride, we were packed like sardines on the deck above the cars. We attempted to sleep slumped in a hallway among crying babies and old men with grizzled chins wearing captain's caps, who smoked and gossiped all night, but it was impossible.

Crete, 225 miles south of the mainland and one of the largest of the Greek islands in the Mediterranean Sea, was warm with blue skies every day. Backpackers were everywhere. Some of them were also living in vans they had bought in Europe, some even living on boats. There were so many "kids" traveling from around the world—American, Canadian, South African, French, Dutch, and New Zealanders. I marveled at how friendly and accepting the village people were. We all parked along the village breakwaters, nearly outnumbering the locals, and bought out the bread in the bakeries. We packed the cafes in the evenings. Alain met Michel, an old fisherman who spoke French. He had fought with the allies in World War II, and he and Alain spent hours visiting, sitting on wooden chairs at tables under the trees near the waterfront.

While walking on the breakwater one day, Alain found an abandoned fishing line with a live fish hooked to it. Actually, there was a bigger fish whose mouth was over a smaller fish that had the fishhook in his mouth. He cleaned the big fish and took it to a cafe where they made it into a big pot of soup. We paid a few pennies more for bread—what a great meal. Life was good.

It was November. We were now in Sitia, a small village on the east end of the island. The American travelers decided to have a Thanksgiving dinner together in the youth hostel compound. There were no turkeys for sale anywhere, so several New England girls hitched a ride to the American army base on the west end of the island to see if they could get access to the PX store. They returned with chickens, twenty pounds of potatoes, and several jars of mincemeat.

I was in charge of the pies. I mixed chopped apples with the mincemeat and raisins, covered it with an oatmeal crumb crust, and carried the two huge pans to the local bakery. The village folks were just as excited about our holiday as we were, and they came to the gate of the hostel in twos and threes with offerings of olives, cucumbers, and tomatoes.

By mid-afternoon, the chickens were roasted and delivered from the bakery. The potatoes were boiled and mashed. Someone had made gravy and dressing. Huge salads and crusty bread were set out. Everyone brought something to sit on from vehicles and boats. Some Californians joined George, a local fisherman, playing guitars and other stringed instruments. A couple of New Hampshire guys dressed up like Indians in headbands and feathers. Village children giggled at the gate. It was a fine Thanksgiving Day.

The van was now much more organized. My Swiss souvenir, a small ski-shaped thermometer, hung from a hook between two of the windows. A candle set into a metal lantern hung over the storage box. My skis took up space against the wall opposite the doors. Under the back seats, we stored the packs, boots, and coats. I kept some yarn and a crochet hook under there too. In the glove compartment we kept maps, books, journals, and pens. A lot of things got moved into the front seat to make more room when we were camping. Every few days we drove out to a beach, emptied the van, swept the floors, and re-sorted everything.

Vai was as far east as we could drive and explore on Crete. There was no village there, just the wilderness and the sea. We parked on the sand under the palms and set up our camp. Alain made fish soup out of some tiny fish he bought from a local fisherman. He expected the bones to cook soft but they didn't and it took work to separate the bones out of each bite. Otherwise it was good soup.

During the night we were startled awake as something heavy scurried across the foot of our sleeping bags. The rest of the night we sat huddled with our feet tucked under us in the center of our plywood platform in the back of the van. Alain was armed and ready with the hatchet. We were quite sure we had several large lizards in the van with us. Dozens more of them tramped heavily on our roof.

At the first rays of dawn, we pulled open our doors, uneasily thumping and shaking everything in order to scare the creatures out. We hated to wake up the British kids camping near us, but we could not rest until we knew what kind of animals had invaded our van. Sleepily, they reassured us the creatures were not gigantic lizards but small palm mice! With heavy, hefty feet, we decided. Battening down, we cranked up the ignition and pointed our stubby car back toward the civilized village of Sitia and souflakis.

George the fisherman wanted to take us fishing. He had a very small wooden boat with a noisy, smoky motor that had just enough room for us to hunker down between the baskets of fishing line. He took the boat out far beyond the land on the rolling seas. Alain's complexion matched the color of the waves—he didn't feel well.

George dropped a Styrofoam buoy with a fishing line attached and doled out the line for more than an hour as the motor slowly trolled the boat along. There were fish hooks fastened from the line every ten or fifteen feet. At last he dropped off the other end of the line tied to the second Styrofoam buoy. We then backtracked to find the first buoy. We were in a miniature boat with a miniscule motor in a huge rough sea with no land in sight searching for a tiny chunk of Styrofoam. He knew what he was doing because it only took a half hour to find it! The line with hundreds of fishhooks was reeled in hand over hand and coiled into the baskets. He had around thirty fish, which was considered a good catch for the day, and he was satisfied. We had been in the boat for six hours. Alain felt worse with each rolling wave, and he was not interested in fishing anymore. Luckily, it was time to head back.

George invited us to spend the evening with him at the waterfront cafe. The cook made us soup from some of George's fish. There were small round crunchy objects in the soup that made a snap when bitten into. I asked George if it was an herb or an unusual seasoning. "No," he said, "it is fish eyes." We were his guests, so I smiled and thanked him. Alain couldn't have looked any greener.

We had heard of the man-made caves carved into the bluffs overlooking the village of Matala on the south coast of Crete, so we headed there one morning, passing through groves and groves of orange trees. The cliffs were as golden and the sea was as blue as the time when pirates, then "beatniks," and later "hippies" lived in the caves. When the village closed and fenced off the caves a few years earlier, the traveling kids moved down into the tiny village, sleeping under the trees, on the beach, and in small buildings. They took over the whole town. When we arrived, it was in sad shape. Garbage and filth were everywhere. Literally dozens of cats prowled for rats.

The small grocery shop was owned by a woman who we all called "Mama." She kept a semblance of order among the travelers. She made sure no one was starving. Gently, with a firm hand, she nudged the drugged-out kids to their feet and hopefully on to responsibility for themselves.

But we felt sad for Matala. The harbor was beautiful, but the beauty had been marred by the self-seeking traveling kids who had overrun the tiny village. I vowed to never find myself in that group. Seeing another village, Agios Gallini, across the harbor, we said good-bye to Mama, and were there in an hour.

It was Christmas. We propped up a branch for a tree and decorated it with yarn pompoms. There were seventeen vans of various makes and shapes owned by travelers parked along the village of Gallini's seawall with the blue Mediterranean Sea stretching south to Africa. A bunch of us played volleyball on the beach every day. I was impressed again with the graciousness of the villagers who welcomed us even though we, as travelers, overtook their city for several weeks, not just for a one-hour tour. Fortunately, in this village the travelers treated the place right, picking up after themselves and showing respect to the villagers.

We parked next to some traveling French Canadian kids whose home was not far from Alain's hometown in Quebec. We spent hours visiting in the sunshine. The girl and I exchanged small gifts—a miniature embroidered fabric bag and a crocheted star for the Christmas tree. Alain gave me a clay candleholder, some oranges, and a frying pan that would fit better on the cookstove. I knitted him a wool scarf, which was not needed in Crete but would come in handy in Quebec, and some mittens, striped maroon and blue of rough local wool.

Just in time for Christmas, I received a cassette tape from my parents filled with messages recorded for me at the annual family reunion. This reminder of home made me think about our holiday traditions. My grandfather would offer the blessing for Christmas dinner. As was his custom, he would also thank God for his nineteen grandchildren and ask for His watch care over each one of us, including me wandering around the world.

That afternoon we visited with a couple who had danced in the film *Jesus Christ Superstar*, which had just finished being filmed in Israel. Tears actually came to their eyes when they described their reaction as they took part in the story of Jesus dying on the cross and rising again. They were on their way back to California and envied our carefree life on the road.

Later Alain and I talked about this unusual conversation, first about the dismay the actors felt over the treatment of Jesus and then their genuine gladness of how the story ended. Alain then admitted that although he had long ago given up on religion he had not given up on believing in God. I was disturbed as I contemplated my years of indifference to this story of Jesus. Later, walking the beach trail alone and feeling a little homesick, I searched for thoughts to mute my uncomfortable and troubling ones.

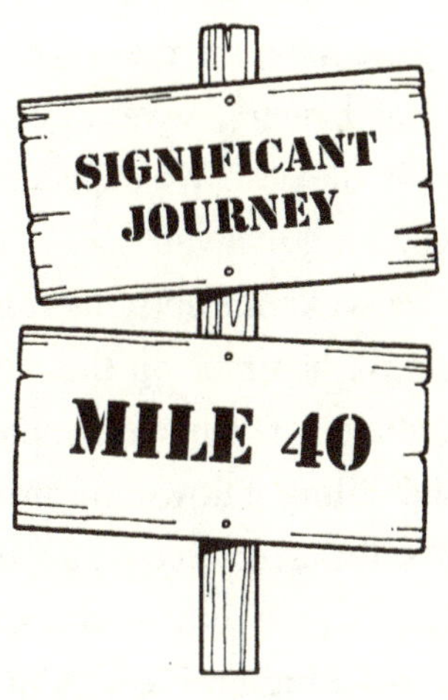

It was Sunday, the last day of 1972. We had been on the road since Thursday, driving east through sleet and snow. We were heading to India. It would be warm there at this time of year. But meanwhile Alain was wearing his scarf and mittens. I had two hats on and was thankful for the long underwear I brought to use for skiing. We hadn't really been warm since leaving Crete, and we still had another day's drive ahead to Istanbul. Because of the cold, we paused only long enough in the cities of Thessalonica and Kavala for fuel and food.

When we passed a sign pointing to the site of Philippi, I remembered a sermon I had heard long ago about Paul praying in prison there. Even when an earthquake made it possible for Paul and his companion to escape, they had stayed, which saved the life of the guard and then changed his life. The point was that Paul not only believed God but he trusted Him, knowing He would be with them no matter what the circumstances. Paul believed God. I believed in God, but did I believe God? Could I ever have that kind of trust? The weather finally broke just before we crossed into Turkey.

The traffic was chaotic in Istanbul. Men on foot, wearing saddles packed high with bags and boxes, competed with trucks, cars, and horse and wagons. One man was carrying a refrigerator on his back. The traffic cops relied heavily on their whistles. We arrived late afternoon, and since it was January, it was already dusk. We parked on a well-lighted four-lane boulevard. We expected such a location to be safer for us, travelers camping in a van.

Around midnight we woke abruptly to someone banging on the van. Someone was using a hammer on the side wing window! The banging stopped immediately when we shouted. We only caught a glimpse of someone hightailing it down the street.

There was only one safe place we could go, the American Embassy. One and a half hours and many wrong directions later we pulled up to the iron gates. But we had a big problem. Alain was a Canadian and couldn't enter. But the Marine guard took mercy after hearing our sad story and let us park in the compound for the remainder of the night.

The next morning bright and early we woke up amidst a fleet of shiny black Mercedes sedans. We were unquestionably the ugly duckling. Later, the consulate directed us to the Blue Mosque and the restaurant called the "Pudding Shop." He said it was the part of Istanbul where we would find a safe place to park with guards and meet fellow travelers who camped in vans. He was friendly and helpful. Before we left he gave us another piece of advice. Do not go into Syria. America did not have relations with this country, and there was no embassy to help us if we ran into trouble. We were just so glad to find out where to park in Istanbul, we didn't think too much more about the rest of his advice.

The next morning a shrill wail startled us out of a very sound sleep while it was still dark. It was our second day in Istanbul, and we were parked across the street from the "Pudding Shop" with several other vans. Four Dutch kids lived in one of them and in another, a load of New Zealanders. We all paid a watchman twenty-five cents for every eight-hour shift.

The wail came from the sky, was amplified, and lasted for about ten minutes. When it got light out, we could see speakers on the mosque turret we were parked directly under, and we quickly learned that this was the Muslim call to prayer. Soon we became accustomed to it, but meanwhile we moved the van a little further from the turret. No wonder that parking space was open!

The "Pudding Shop" was more than a cafe. It was our depository of knowledge, not just about Turkey and Istanbul but also about the countries ahead of us as far east as India, Pakistan, and Nepal. We sat at a table over tea every evening exchanging experiences, advice, and warnings. Istanbul was the gateway to the East, and we soaked up all the helpful information.

Nepal, after India, was our ultimate goal, but we would go as far as Afghanistan for sure. On the map it wasn't that far, closer than Los Angeles was to New York. As long as I was with Alain, this arduous destination seemed possible. Not only did he have an aptitude for showing confidence in any situation but he confessed he would not want to travel with anyone besides me. And I couldn't imagine seeing more of the world with anyone other than him. Besides, I had an Afghan hound at home waiting for me, being cared for by friends, so I was intrigued about seeing the country where this breed of dog originated. We had the time, and gas was a lot cheaper then in Europe. So that was where we would go when we were ready to leave Istanbul.

One day a huge olive-green truck with double tires and a small cab-like turret minus the guns on its rooftop pulled up and parked beside us—it was obviously a remodeled military vehicle. A German kid stepped down. He was heading east to India. This was his sixth trip. He bought jackets and dresses in Afghanistan, India, and Nepal and took them back to Germany to sell. The rest of us travelers were all in awe of his truck, insulated against the cold weather, set up with water tanks, carrying enough motor parts and tools to rebuild his entire engine if need be. He also carried an entire new set of tires and appeared to be so well-equipped and well-stocked that he could spend a winter in Siberia or a summer on the Sahara. When he asked us where we were headed, we mumbled something about down the road. We were embarrassed to say "Afghanistan." We carried only a screwdriver and a bald spare tire.

The bazaars of Istanbul in January were great. Tourists were few and merchants, anxious for business, bargained straightforwardly. Alain traded his tattered jeans directly off his body for a couple pairs of corduroy pants. We traded the backseat of the van for cash plus a couple of wooden boxes to hold up the plywood platform. The plywood was always bouncing around on the seat springs and the new boxes gave us more storage space. Whenever we were in the van, locals would stop and ask to buy anything, especially items removable from the car like the mirrors, steering wheel, even the gearshift! But we figured selling the backseat was about the most we should capitalize on this bonanza.

With the cash, we bought a Cashmere goat skin, custom-made suede jackets, and one-inch Styrofoam panels to insulate the bare metal van walls against the cold and condensation.

It took us most of a day to cut the Styrofoam to fit on the ceiling and walls of the car. We tried to fasten it in place with a white water-based glue first, spending hours on our backs holding it up with our feet, only to have it fall when we let go, the glue still wet. The whole day struck us as pretty funny, feet sticking up in the air holding up the ceiling. But then most days we spent laughing together.

We needed a plan B. Model airplane cement ate the Styrofoam, but we discovered that the trick was to put it only on the van walls and let it begin to set before plastering the Styrofoam sheets against it. We also found that it was important to cut the Styrofoam into small pieces to lessen the pull of the weight. The van resembled a mono-color mosaic when we were finished, but with the curtains pulled and wearing layers of clothing, we were warmer. Plus, condensation no longer dripped onto us when it warmed up inside.

We gratefully paid our twenty-five cents to the night watchman. He was very loyal and chased people away when he saw us tiring of their hassle. One cold snowy evening, we felt sorry for him standing outside, puffing on his hands to keep warm, so we invited him in for some hot tea.

Before we left Istanbul, everyone said that we should try a Turkish bath, and since we found one that said seventy cents, we gave it a try. On the women's side, I was handed a towel and a small porcelain bowl and was directed to a changing booth. The instructions were written on the wall in Turkish, so I was not sure of the procedure. I just followed a hall to a huge vaulted domed room. This was an old Roman bath, hundreds of years old. Along the walls at intervals were spigots and marble basins built low into the wall, close to the floor. There were several other occupants in the room. I copied them, lathering and rinsing my hair using the spigot and bowl. Through the steam I could see the rich centuries-old mosaics, but I decided that I much preferred a clean shower spray after all.

As soon as we could get our visas, we planned to head to Lebanon. In order to obtain our visas, we were required to get vaccinated for cholera. The clinic was crowded, and it opened directly off a busy, dirty street. No one spoke English. I wrote the word "cholera" on a piece of paper and handed that along with my international health card to the woman at the desk. The nurse pulled a glass syringe and non-disposable needle out of a metal tray filled with liquid. The needle was so dull she had to jab twice to get it in my arm, making me question whether the shot was really necessary. Later when we entered a country where there was a cholera epidemic, we decided that the jabs were worth it.

A French kid carrying no bags and wearing only sandals with slouching gray socks wanted a ride to Beirut. About that time an English guy wearing granny glasses and carrying a dingy backpack stopped us in the "Pudding Shop" with the same request. Our visas were ready. It was time to leave and head south to warmer weather. We decided to make this as business-like as possible, so we briskly requested that they meet us in the parking lot under the Blue Mosque at 7:30 sharp in the morning to depart for Lebanon.

By eight in the morning, the icy roads were softening, so we headed across the city with our passengers perched on the plywood in back. We were headed to the bridge we could see from the Blue Mosque—the bridge that crossed the channel into Asia. After fighting the morning traffic for an hour, we arrived to find the bridge was closed. But not just closed, it was not even completely constructed! Yes, it had all of its cables, pillars, and posts, but the road bed itself was empty space! From a distance, it looked like a complete bridge. Our riders were slightly annoyed, but it struck us as funny.

We threaded our way back through the hundreds of taxis and trucks to the ferry docks, which were within shouting distance from where we had started that morning. Around two in the afternoon, we finally set foot on the Asian side for the first time.

Snow had begun to fall. The roads were filled with potholes. The afternoon was dim, and it was quickly getting dimmer. We hadn't eaten since before we picked up our passengers. Our riders did not want to stop and eat. They were running out of patience. They wanted to make some mileage before nightfall. Besides, they had been snacking in the back all day, so of course they weren't hungry.

We had only gone a few miles. If it hadn't been for the low clouds, we could probably have still seen the buildings of Istanbul. But there was a café, and we needed some hot soup. Our passengers sat, scowling, only faintly speaking when spoken to while we ate. It was nice and warm inside. If we were not encumbered with paying riders, we would have camped right there in front of the cafe, but they insisted that we push on. I was wondering if they expected to arrive in Beirut by nightfall.

In the parking lot, we found our van covered with two inches of new snow and sporting a very flat tire. Our passengers were no longer happy campers, and they did not speak, at least to us. We pulled out our jack and spare tire, but we soon discovered that we did not have a tire wrench! And to confuse things a little more, the jack we did have was not the right one for our van! The snow began to fall thick and fast. Daylight dwindled. Our riders were downright surly as they left to catch a train. Our day as public transport had ended before it really began. It struck us both as pretty hilarious. I was glad that we could laugh on such a very cold January day.

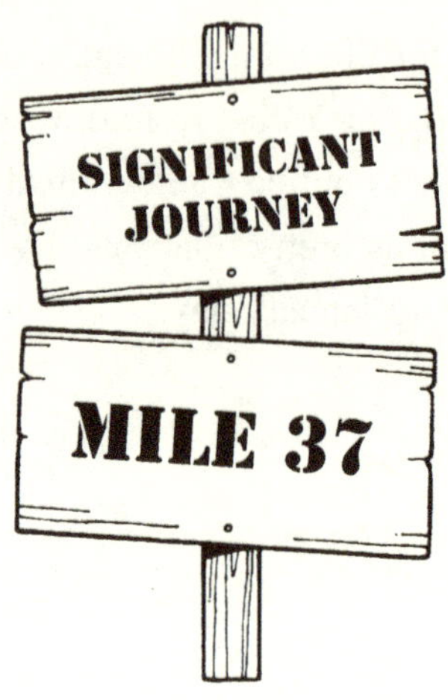

We were stranded on a high plateau in central Turkey. Groups of people were leading sheep for sacrifices. It was some sort of four-day holiday, and the banks were closed, which left us no where to cash our traveler's checks. We, two scruffy North Americans, were without cash for gas or food. But a kindhearted shop girl loaned us one hundred Turkish lira so we could buy groceries and continue on our way. She will never know how much she uplifted our spirits that dismal day. We traveled for about a hundred miles when we found the banks open again, so we stopped and mailed her a thank-you note with our repayment.

A day or so later we hit a turkey in Turkey. Really! We had been making good time, but that slowed us down a little bit. We were anxious to drop off the frozen plateau and follow the south coast on the Mediterranean Sea where we could finally warm up. But meanwhile, near the village of Emisdag, we parked for the night next to a police or military compound since it seemed like a safe place.

All evening people brought us things. First soup and bread, then a bag of tangerines, hot tea, olives, and even blankets! We were puzzled by their kind deeds, which was beyond common hospitality.

By morning we understood their concern. It was so cold that frost had formed on our sleeping bags from our breath, and all the metal inside the van was frosted. The windows were completely frozen. The doors were even frozen shut! It seemed as if half the village was outside to greet us when we broke out. Smiling, they offered us more olives, bread, and hot tea—they were obviously relieved we had survived the night. Our thermometer registered five below zero degrees Fahrenheit.

The engine of our van whined in the high altitude and cold of the central plateau of Turkey. The sound brought back memories of my dad. Every morning before he left for work, he sat in his easy chair, running his electric razor over his chin, reading his Bible. That was a very comforting scene to me growing up. My parents had been so good about not pestering me about my lack of connection with Christianity, but I knew that they were sad about it.

We traveled through the village of Konya where women were wearing bright-colored Turkish trousers. Here, thousands of feet above sea level it was so cold. The sun shone weakly and could not break through the frozen air. As we dropped down to the Turkish Riviera, the air softened and the surrounding groves were full of oranges and lemons. Camels carried boxes of fruit tied to their sides, and little boys balanced water jugs on burros. We were warm again.

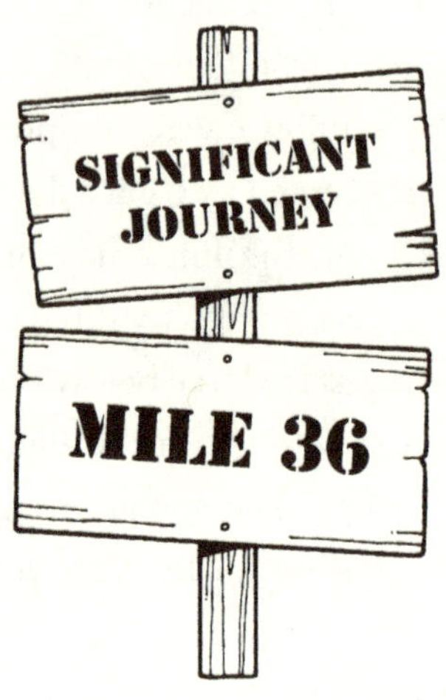

The kind American consulate in Istanbul had advised us not to go into Syria, but we faced a big problem. We had to cross over part of Syria to get to Lebanon. There was no other way to do it. In preparation for our crossing, I had written to the American consulate in Beirut telling them of our plans, the date we were expecting to arrive in Beirut, and the address of my parents. That way they would know who to contact if I didn't report into the Beirut office on time and turned up missing. It seemed like a responsible thing to do at the time.

Fortunately, our trip across Syria was uneventful. Once we arrived in Beirut, we drove straight to the American Embassy to report in. I let them know that we were safe after driving through northern Syria, and I emphasized the need to destroy my earlier communication to them.

Weeks later I learned that the American Embassy did not process my second message. The State Department in Washington D.C. contacted my parents via phone and informed them that their daughter had not checked into the Lebanese Embassy after crossing through Syria. Had they heard from her? My folks had not. Thankfully, the very next day my postcard arrived from Beirut. Their hearts returned to a normal beat, but the new gray in their hair was permanent.

We applied for Jordan, Iraq, and Iran visas at the various embassies, but we discovered that there was no American Embassy in Baghdad. I had asked my family at home and friends in Europe to send any Christmas mail to a non-existent address! Someone somewhere in Baghdad enjoyed all of the small gifts and letters sent to me there.

We lived like royalty in Beirut. It was a modern, beautiful city with whitewashed buildings shimmering beside the sea. We parked on the waterfront seawall near the five-star hotels and used the lobby bathrooms, trying to inconspicuously wash our hair and socks in the sinks. It was so good to see regular American-style toilet paper again and nice soap! A western-dressed businessman came by our van daily to practice his English. In exchange for our instruction, he helped us get two new tires and treated us to a good restaurant meal. The weather was nice and sunny. We set up our lawn chairs on the seawall and enjoyed the sea breeze and easy life.

One day as we sat in the sun, police chased a group of students past us, beating those they caught with their billy sticks. We realized that peace was a facade on this glowing white city. Up high on the bluff across from where we sat, soldiers with machine guns were silhouetted against the blue sky. Here and there we caught glimpses of the turmoil bubbling just below the surface in this country. We saw people, thousands of them, packed tightly into tents and shacks on vacant city blocks midst the high-rise office buildings. Someone told us that they were Palestinian refugees who had been displaced for more than twenty years.

These troubling scenes stuck in my mind one day and brought unsettling thoughts about my own life that persisted the rest of the afternoon. When did I fall away from living a life that included God? It was so gradual. I had considered invitations to parties where there was dancing and drinking as opportunities to witness. Besides, it was fun to be with my friends, and I was flattered by the attention. Armed with all the biblical facts about healthy Christian living and being a staunch, strong person, I didn't think I would have any trouble holding on to my faith in any circumstance.

At first I kept up a pretense of the Christian life with my family, attending church, even taking part in the programs, but eventually it took too much energy. My own strength wasn't enough. It had been years, at least six years, since I took that first step away, but was that really the first step. Or had I never been truly connected to God in the first place? I didn't want to think about this now, so I brushed my questions aside.

In spite of the unsettling scenes of the refugee camps, we found Beirut to be a sparkling exotic jewel in the Middle East. We discovered peanut butter in the stores and decided this may have some impact on our impression. One day a young boy in baggy trousers wearing a turban stopped with his camera and asked in French if he could snap our photo. Hey, who was the picturesque one here? Alain's Quebec-accented French climbed over the language barrier, and we learned fast about the culture.

Every day we walked the boulevards looking in the boutique windows and buying groceries in western-style stores. But after a couple of weeks, this sort of life began to wear on us, so with our visas in hand, we left Beirut early one sunny afternoon heading east up into and over the hills behind the city. There were few views as spectacular as the view down through the Lebanese cedars of Beirut glowing in the sunshine.

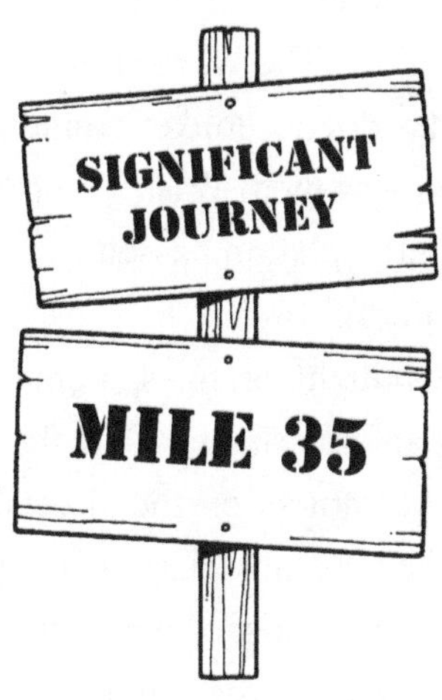

Baalbeck was a quiet village with a few ancient ruins but many small boys anxious to show us the sites. We had learned from our "travel authorities" at the "Pudding Shop" in Istanbul to steer clear of any invitations in Baalbeck. Traveling kids were an easy mark, and accepting invitations to dinner or to visit would obligate us to our hosts to buy drugs. And they expected North Americans to be big spenders.

After wandering through the ruins and taking photos of camels, we drove on. Since we got into no trouble on our first sprint across Syria to get to Lebanon, we considered ourselves experts and able to make a second sprint across that country to get to Jordan. We parked just before the border and woke the next morning in a thunderstorm with six inches of new snow. So we put our hiking boots and winter socks back on.

Damascus! It hit me that I was standing where people in the Bible had stood. I said to myself, "Here I am standing in Damascus!"

That barren winter afternoon when I saw the sign saying "Damascus, 5 Km," I remembered the story of the man named Saul who centuries ago had entered this same city not far from our same route. He lost his sight there and wouldn't have seen the sheep grazing on the brown hillsides, the mud huts, or the robed and turbaned man trudging along the shoulder. The woman in black holding a large jar in the doorway and the docile donkey standing quietly beside the well were much the same as then. Wasn't he running away from God too? My moment of contemplation passed as we pulled to a stop on a muddy street in the center of town.

In the market we bought oranges, potatoes, and apples while staring at all the animal parts hanging in the meat vendors' stalls. There were no other Westerners on the streets. We expected to feel fearful, but we didn't. For the most part the people were indifferent to our presence, but not hostile. Most of the young men were in uniform. Many of the children were also wearing military green.

We stayed just long enough to get the kinks out of our legs before heading south, passing many trucks and tanks upturned on the side of the road. We didn't know if this was the result of some recent skirmish with Israel or poor driving habits. There were what appeared to be fox holes dug here and there, some big enough to hide trucks, but they could have been bomb craters. The road was narrow with no shoulders, crossing miles and miles of flat land covered with black shiny rocks that matched the wrecks along the way.

At the Jordanian border, we endured a thorough search of our van and of our persons. I was taken into a small makeshift room where a woman searched me. Alain was searched on the spot in the roadway. But that was not the worst. We discovered that we didn't have the proper papers for the van to enter Jordan. It was hours later and nearing midnight when this problem was pointed out to us.

Just then a jeep pulled up beside us and the uniformed driver motioned for us to get in the backseat. Were they taking us to jail? Confused but not wanting to cause a scene, we climbed in. The jeep entered the gate into Jordan and drove slowly through the sleeping streets of the adjacent village, stopping in front of a large home with darkened windows. The driver motioned us to follow him up the walkway where he knocked on the carved wooden door. Lights switched on and a tousle-headed but stately man, obviously in nightclothes, opened it.

He listened politely to the officer, his eyes held unblinking on us as we stood slightly trembling off to the side. He signed a paper handed to him, and with a quick nod of his head, quietly closed the door. The officer turned, motioned us back into the jeep, and drove back to the border. After taking the signed paper, the border patrol waved us through into Jordan with a smile. The man in the pajamas was the official who signed for cars entering Jordan.

The next morning we drove through the Jerash ruins and on to Amman. There we saw the American flag at the Embassy flying at half-mast. Former President Johnson had passed away. All things North American seemed very remote as we made our way through the robed masses. But the sun was shining, and we were warm once again. We headed south on what is called the Desert Highway to the coastal village of Aqaba, passing grazing camels, Bedouin tents, and flocks of sheep.

On the way we stopped on the edge of a plateau with a panoramic view below us of odd peaks and hills rising directly from the flat valley floor. We didn't know until later that this was Lawrence of Arabia's country, Wadi Rum, where the battles were fought and where the film of the same name was made. Later in Aqaba we met a man who still had the robe costume he wore as an extra in the movie. He was proud of his photo with Omar Sharif, the movie star, and brought it out whenever we stopped by his shop.

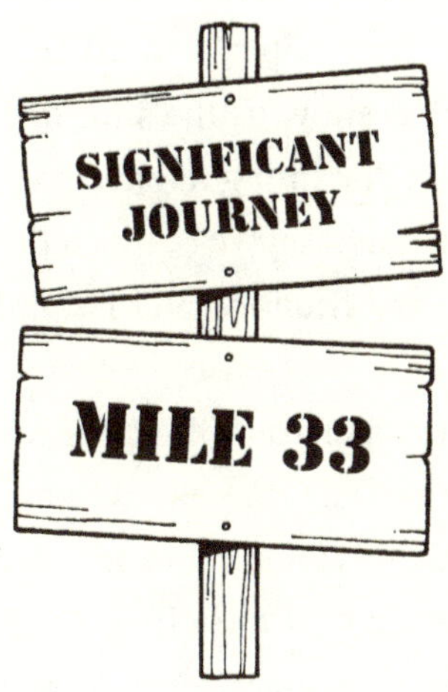

Every second person seemed to be wearing a military uniform in Aqaba on the Red Sea. A short distance down the beach, we walked up to a wire fence where we could look into Israel. This was definitely a border town.

Soldiers became a part of our life. They were the first people we saw in the morning, lounging around our camp as we brushed our teeth, looking into our pots of food as they simmered, and checking the fabric of our jackets. We were the objects of observation all day long, but we made a point to be friendly, even taking the time to show them more closely what we were doing. If I was making soup, I showed them the inside of my pot before they came to look. If I was reading, I got up and showed them any pictures or illustrations.

One night after we pulled the curtains and were eating dinner, we were aware of subtle movements outside our windows. For the fun of it, Alain yanked the curtains open suddenly, startling three men so much that they fell over each other.

Our every move seemed intriguing to the locals. We didn't know if it was because not many travelers camped there or because we were the only travelers around. We had seen very few tourists in Jordan.

Most likely it was because we were what people would call "hippies." At least we were not under military surveillance.

Villagers clamored to show us the sites or invite us to a relative's restaurant. At first it was disarming to have so much attention, and we were slightly defensive, but then we realized that the Jordanian people were simply curious, very friendly, and helpful. And they wanted to practice their English.

In the palms on the waterfront of Aqaba where we were camping, there was a lot of foot traffic. One day we saw a quiet section of the beach curving southeast toward Arabia and decided to spend the day there. We drove to the edge of the village, but we discovered that a tollgate blocked the roadway guarded by a small, but stout uniformed man. We smiled, motioning that we would like to go through. He spoke rapidly, but motioned no entrance. However, he returned our smiles. Exchanging his smile, we motioned that we would like to swim on the beach. Speaking in a friendly but firm voice, he shook his head no.

It was so hot and dusty and those blue waves lapping lazily on the sand just a short distance ahead of us were so inviting. We got out of the car, shook his hand, and again pantomimed that we wanted to go swimming in the water. We indicated that we would be happy to help him lift the pole blocking our way. He paused, smiled again, shrugged, and then, without further ado, lifted the pole so that we could go through. At dusk when we returned, the guard smiled at us and waved us through. Every day we went through the same charade before he lifted the pole and let us pass through the gate.

Sitting on the beach we claimed as our own brought back memories of Bible stories I had grown up with. We were on the Red Sea. Moses and the children of Israel traveled across the bay on their way to the Promised Land. God was with them even when they didn't care or comprehend it. How long does He wait for those who are not ready to be His followers? I pondered.

The sun shone, a slight breeze wafted off the water, and a herd of camels grazed nearby. Alain was snorkeling, and I lounged in the lawn chair in the shade of the van reading. Occasionally I glanced across the blue Red Sea and wondered where Moses and the children of Israel had passed. A turbaned man came by leading a camel, and I talked him into a ride. He demonstrated the sounds he made to signal his camel to kneel, rise, or turn.

Except for the miltary green jeeps, the occasional tank, and the soldiers who appeared out of thin air, we and the camels had the beach to ourselves. If I gazed directly up into the cliffs to the east, I saw a number of large cannon-type guns pointing over my head toward Israel, a half mile across the bay to the west.

It was about a week later when we decided to drive south on our sandy beach road a few short miles to look across the border into Arabia. A truck with machine guns stopped us within sight of the border buildings. By then we had figured out that our private beach area was some sort of military zone. We didn't know it at that time, but not long after our quiet days on this beach, there was an all-out war.

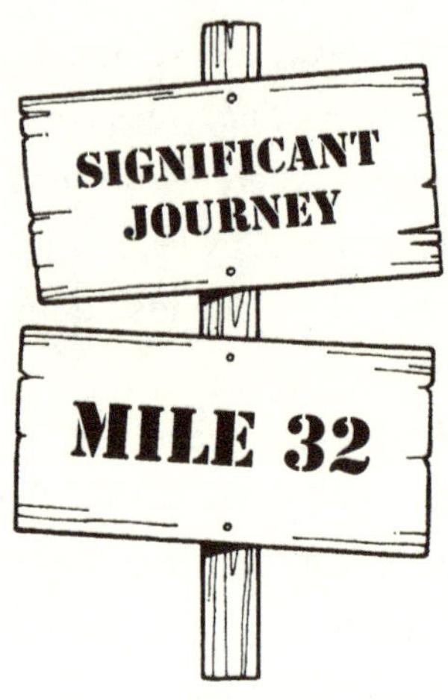

In Aqaba we met Fouad. He was a small Arab who worked for the big hotel on the waterfront. Interestingly enough, he rode a donkey to work. We called him "Little Big Man." He rented snorkels and swim fins to us at prices that fit our budget. But the best thing was the showers he rented us for a quarter. He showed real interest in our welfare, and we went to visit with him every day. He became a true friend.

The coral and fish were beautiful in the shallow water. Because it was so nice in Aqaba, we decided to stay for awhile. We thought it would be fun to have a pet cat, but even with Fouad's help, we had no luck catching one of the many wild ones near his hotel. Later, on a tiny side street, Alain found a batch of kittens. The lady standing in the doorway was amused at our interest and gladly handed one over to us. We called the cat Geritol, but we eventually took him back because he never adjusted to being held or petted.

On Valentine's Day, when looking for something special to cook for dinner, we came across a chicken store. Cages of clucking white-feathered chickens were stacked to the ceiling. Thinking these live chickens were just part of the store's advertising, and expecting the shopkeeper to pull one out of a freezer, we bought one. But instead, in front of our astonished eyes, he yanked a chicken out of a cage, slit its' throat, cleaned it, plucked the feathers, and handed it over to us by its' feet, all in a matter of minutes! We had lost our appetite and couldn't cook or eat it. So we gave it away and bought a candy bar and a chunk of cheese, which went just as well with a big pan of fried spuds and onions.

Another day we were on our way to a restaurant to have fish soup when we met two men who earlier in the afternoon had been hanging around our van. Alain had told them that I didn't speak English because I was a North American Indian, hoping they would tire and leave. At the restaurant the one who spoke good English mentioned how quiet, "like an Indian" I was.

"How do you say 'Good Morning' in your language?" he asked me.

"I'm shy," I replied. Then quickly remembering I wasn't supposed to be able to understand, I lowered my head.

"What did she say?" he asked Alain.

"She's shy," Alain replied.

"Oh, Shee-shy! OK, so then, how do you say, "Good Afternoon?"

"Shee-Shee," I replied. It just slipped out.

On the road just north of Aqaba, we pulled into a guesthouse parking lot with a sign directing to a place called Petra. Except for an Italian couple in the cafe there, we were the only foreigners. We had no idea what Petra was, but we hiked through a gorge the next morning to find out.

From the first glimpse of the building called "Treasury," which was carved out of the rouge stone face of a cliff wall, to our view from the huge vault of a door of the building called the "Monastery," we marveled and wondered and were amazed and dazed at the wonderful sights. Who knew about this place? When had it been discovered? We had never heard about it before!

The trails went on and on. It was just us and the Bedouins. We hiked all day, exploring the small valleys and canyons, climbing to the tops of rocks and cliffs, finding more and more carved buildings. Bedouins were living in them, cooking over fires built in the entrances, hanging their washed clothes in the bushes by the doorways. Children were tending their goat and sheep flocks, filling their plastic water jugs in the creeks, and riding their donkeys to clumps of pasture amid the ruins. Young Bedouin girls hid their faces and scrambled off the trails as we passed them.

It was a day spent a thousand years back in time. I was convinced no one knew about this place. It was not until we were back in North America that we read more about Petra, that spectacular rose red city that flourished in the second and third centuries, BC. And no, we were not the first people to discover it!

On the hike out at dusk, two young boys offered us free rides on their horses. It was dark when we arrived at our van. We said good-bye to our little Bedouin friends and handed over the horses. The whole day had had a dream-like quality about it.

The next day we started driving up what was called the King's Highway, heading north to Amman where we were going to try and find a way to enter Israel. Along this highway there were tents pitched next to bridges where uniformed watchmen stayed. Even some of the orchards had tents pitched in them. Except for the military trucks wrapped in camouflage netting, we were the only ones driving that road.

We passed through pretty villages with tattoo-faced women in rich black gowns with embroidered edges in bright colors wearing plastic sandals. Men sauntered along the road fingering strings of beads in their hands. Children all waved at us. Many horses grazed in the fields and the apple trees were in blossom.

We dropped into a gorge called Wadi Musa. It was a spectacular place, and the van churned slowly down the winding road to the bottom before starting the climb out. The whole thing, which looked similar to the Grand Canyon, took at least an hour to negotiate.

Just outside the next village, a policeman waved us to a stop. He wanted to check our papers. Our visas were missing an official stamp giving us permission to stay in Jordan longer than two weeks. Even though it was our responsibility to get this stamp and we were now illegally in Jordan, the kind police officer apologized to us for the inconvenience of stopping us and set our passports in order. His navy helmet with a silver spike on the top bobbed and nodded as he smiled and sent us on our way. I wanted to take a photo of him and his hat, but he had already been overly generous.

A short distance further we were flagged down by another policeman, but this time he wanted to ask us if we would be willing to provide transportation to a Bedouin policeman and his wife. The Bedouin's uniform was a long khaki wool robe with a red leather belt banded across his chest, sword and all. His young wife shyly peeked sideways at me from beneath a colorful headscarf. I could hardly contain myself to be sitting beside two such exotic people and wished with all my heart that we spoke the same language. We traveled thirty kilometers before I was able to communicate my question to the husband through hand motions. "What is your name?"

We turned toward the Dead Sea at the village of Karak. At the first of several checkpoints, we discovered we were supposed to have special permission from an office in Amman to go to the Dead Sea. I asked if they could please just let us go down to have a look. We would come right back up the same road. Again the Jordanian soldiers gave in, opened the gates, and let us pass. But at the last gate the soldier was much more firm and refused to let us go on. I pleaded with him, telling him that I had come thousands of miles just to see the Dead Sea and take a photo of it.

"What was that, about a photo?" he asked.

"I just want to take a photo, then we will come right back."

"No photos allowed! This is a military zone, and you are not supposed to be here. No Cameras! Give it to me," he said as he reached into the car.

It was hot out. There was no breeze. In fact the air seemed heavy and weighed me down, taking all of my energy with it. I was tired, and as he paused and peered intently into my face, I felt tears of frustration forming at the corners of my eyes.

"Well, OK, go, but come right back!'" he softened, not mentioning my camera again.

We hiked across fields, through weeds and brush and finally reached the Dead Sea. We took pictures and put our hands into the water before turning and retracing our steps. We reached the van, and as our vehicle labored up the hills to the high plateau above, I wondered where Sodom and Gomorrah had been located.

Later, we stopped in a small village and I ventured into an open-fronted shop. The little shop was filled with gunnysacks standing on end, tops rolled open like fat sleeves, filled with lentils, rice, and other things. The light was poor. Intent on my errand, sorting through some onions and eggs, I was only faintly aware that it felt crowded. When I entered the shop, it had been empty. I straightened up and glanced around. People, large and small, were crowded around me, watching and observing me, talking and discussing me as they pressed in closer and closer. The shop wasn't more than ten or twelve feet wide, and there must have been at least twenty-five or thirty people in there!

It overwhelmed me after all those days with soldiers watching me wash my face, peering into the van windows, and fingering my sleeves. Suddenly I felt the dry dusty heat and smelled the tightness of too many people. It was too much. Spinning around, I raised my hands to my ears and flapped them like wings as I jumped toward the crowd yelling, "SCRAM, SCRAM!" They quickly scattered, spilling out the open doorway. A soldier just a few yards down the road saw the mass exodus and trotted up double time, peering into the shop as he slid to a stop. My first thought was, Oh no, now I'm in trouble!

Instead, catching his breath, he apologized to me for the villagers' behavior and then he stood guard. He smilingly stayed in the shop entrance while I finished shopping, now with plenty of elbow room. I gave him a grateful smile as I carried my bag away.

Imagine our surprise when we found a way into Israel! Every traveler we had spoken to on this journey had told us that because of the political situation, the only way from the Middle East was to fly to Cyprus then into Israel. But on a five-dollar-a-day budget, this expensive route was out of the question. We found a man in a travel agency in Amman, the capital city of Jordan, who arranged for us to go on a "tour" of Israel, but, he explained, it would be very important for us not to get an Israeli stamp on our passports. The stamp would prevent us from re-entering Jordan.

The International Hotel in Amman had a big parking lot, so we left the van there hoping that no one would notice it. Of course this was a futile hope since ours was the only vehicle that was not a Mercedes. On top of that, it was at least fifteen years older then any other car there. It probably would have helped to remove the words "Belly Button Bomb" from across the front, but we didn't think of that.

With packs on our backs, we met the taxi that took us on a horrifically fast ride down to the Jordan River and dropped us off among the Palestinians to sit and wait for something to happen.

Eventually, they loaded us into a rickety old bus, which carried us across the river, all thirty feet of it, and deposited us on the Israeli side.

"Passport please," I was brusquely asked in California-accented English by the officer leaning over a record book at the long table.

"You have to promise not to stamp it," I requested.

"Passport please!" Not looking up, the uniformed man repeated firmly.

"You have to promise not to stamp it, or I can't get back into Jordan where I left my car," I repeated desperately.

"The last time I made a promise it was to my wife, and I've regretted it ever since. Passport please!" replied the official who looked up without cracking a smile. I volunteered that he could put the stamp on a separate piece of paper as a souvenir for me, but he refused. No stamp and no smile. But I saw a twinkle in his eye.

Five hours after leaving Amman in Jordan, we were in Jerusalem, forty miles away. There we meandered around, marveling at how modern it seemed after Jordan. It was disappointing to me to see the biblical landmarks so commercialized and looking nothing like I imagined. But to Alain, raised a Catholic, he knew it would mean a great deal to his parents that he had been there. So in the markets, he found a beautiful Rosary out of olive wood for his mother.

Although the tourist crowds were distracting as they swarmed around the designated holy sites in Jerusalem and Bethlehem, I was struck with the realization that so many people from all around the world came here because they believed in Jesus. I knew that Jesus was real, too, but why didn't that fact make any difference in my life?

At the cathedral, which was supposedly the site where Jesus was born, it was difficult to imagine a rough manger. But at the garden tomb it was easy to envision Jesus walking out of the grave. It hit me, it is a real place! I had never thought of Jesus being that real, but He died, was buried here, and rose again. What did it all mean for me? For a few moments these thoughts pressed down on me. But since there was so much to see and do, I didn't trouble myself with finding an answer at that moment.

Our van was waiting for us when we returned to the hotel parking lot in Jordan. Heading east toward Baghdad, Iraq, we crossed a parched desert plain broken at long intervals with scrubby palm oases. We passed camel herds and Bedouin tents, and we met a couple of Americans on motorcycles when we stopped to camp. They had been to India and were on their way back. The first question travelers always asked after "Where are you headed?" was "Do you have any books to trade?" I got two new books to read in exchange for *The Caravan* by James Michener, which someone had traded me on Crete.

It was cold and the road was very rough. There was very little traffic on the highway, but a rock from a passing truck hit our windshield and cracked it. Seventy kilometers further on, a bus passed us and the whole windshield blew out into our laps, covering us with small chunks of glass. We were not hurt, but it was hard to drive with the wind streaming in. We wrapped our faces in scarves and drove on.

Dusk was falling just as we entered Baghdad, and it was right then that the gas pedal stopped working. We coasted to a stop in front of what appeared to be some sort of institution, perhaps an embassy. A Catholic priest came out with a smile on his face, and after assessing our damages, he gave us directions to the auto shops for in the morning. A few minutes later, he returned with a box overflowing with candle stubs. We felt safe for the night in front of this place even though our windshield was gone. He assured us that they would watch out for us.

The next morning we found a windshield for the van. There were dozens of small shops on the same street where workers were rebuilding from scratch all makes and models of cars, some at least thirty years old. Including the installation, our windshield and gas pedal wire cost only ten American dollars. Even with the time it took for some helpful men to push us over to the shop, everything was fixed by noon.

This concrete city was full of bikes and crowds of men. Most were indifferent to us, but there were some unfriendly faces. I am sure it was because I was not covered from head to foot including my face, which was the custom of the women. We stayed long enough to head south to the site of Babylon where we camped overnight next to the ruins.

At daylight we surveyed our surroundings. We could see that the site was fairly small and was mostly unfenced and open to the surrounding countryside. After walking under a big archway embossed with two-dimensional lions, we found a small building off to one side that housed a couple of artifact cases and a robed man to whom we paid a small fee. There was another building, newly constructed of ancient design, with more lions embossed on its mud brick surface. We could not find an entrance.

Daniel had lived there. I wondered aloud about where the lion's den and the fiery furnace were located. This was where Nebuchadnezzar had had his dream of a metal and clay statue. Alain had never heard these stories from the Bible, so I told them to him.

We wandered up onto a hill of rubble and sat, gazing down into a partially excavated room. An older man showed up who spoke a bit of

English and explained that we were looking at the banquet hall where the writing on the wall took place. The writing on the wall—wasn't it a warning to the people of this very city where we were standing, a warning about the last chance to change their way of life? This was once a great metropolis, but now it was a pile of debris.

My thoughts were sober as I watched the silhouettes of three boys in billowing robes playing on a mound of dust-covered broken bricks against the morning sun. A dog slinked around a rock pile as we headed back to the van. I leaned down and picked up a broken brick with hieroglyphics on the side. "Perhaps it says made by the Babylonian Brick Company," I mused.

Except for a couple of French kids in a compact car, we were the only visitors that day. As we pulled away, I took one more look back at the lion archway. There was a lot that had happened at this ancient site. Some day when I had time, I wanted to read about it again. Right then, we had many miles to go before we rested, so we headed back north.

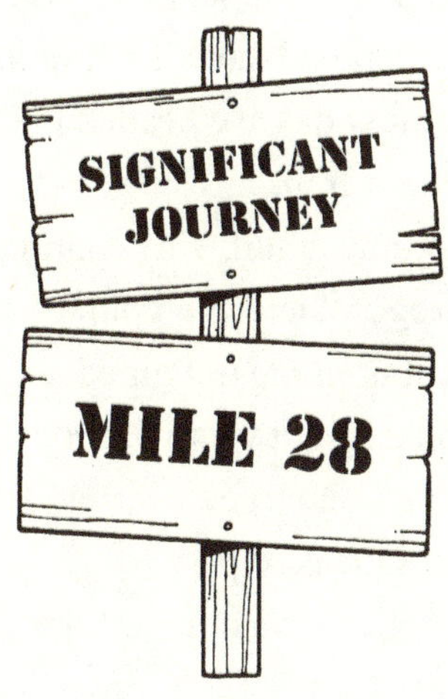

The Iranian border was coming up. We passed factory after factory where they made tiles and bricks. They resembled gigantic ovens with tall chimneys. Again, like we saw in Syria, there were acres and acres of black shiny rock. Since the dwellings were made out of native materials, they blended into their surroundings. A few times we saw a black camel in the many herds wandering around. Horses pulling wagons were delivering kerosene. Once in awhile we passed red-haired people with blue eyes, the women in bright clothing and uncovered heads. The men were wearing bloomer pants and moving energetically. Later we learned that these were the Kurdish people.

We crossed into Iran with a minimum of fuss. There were as many pedestrians, usually walking down the middle of the streets, as there were vehicles. Drivers entering the main highway didn't usually look; they just pulled out.

We arrived in Tehran late in the afternoon and found our way to the American Express office. We also planned to apply for Afghani visas in Tehran, but everything was closed. This was a city of four million people. It was so hot and muggy and the traffic was so bad that we parked next to a huge monument and bought some ice cream bars from a turbaned cart vendor. The wrappers had printed on them "Canada Frost," which we folded up and saved, a fragment of familiarity in a sea of strangeness. The next day we headed north over the mountains toward Mashad in northern Iran.

Every vehicle, large and small, was continually passing, as if we were all playing leapfrog. Where the country was flat and visibility was good, this was OK, but in the unlighted, curved, potholed tunnels going north to the Caspian Sea, it was a different story. A bus passed us in one such tunnel with a huge truck bearing down from the opposite direction. Somehow we squeaked past.

Another thing we noticed was that all the trucks seemed to have their exhaust pipes spewing smoke at our window level. The roads were generally in better repair than in Iraq, but they were only wide enough to pass oncoming traffic safely if one vehicle dropped onto the shoulder, which didn't always exist. It was a game of "chicken" to see who would pull one wheel off the road. Going by the number of overturned buses and trucks along the sides of the road, it looked like plenty of them had lost.

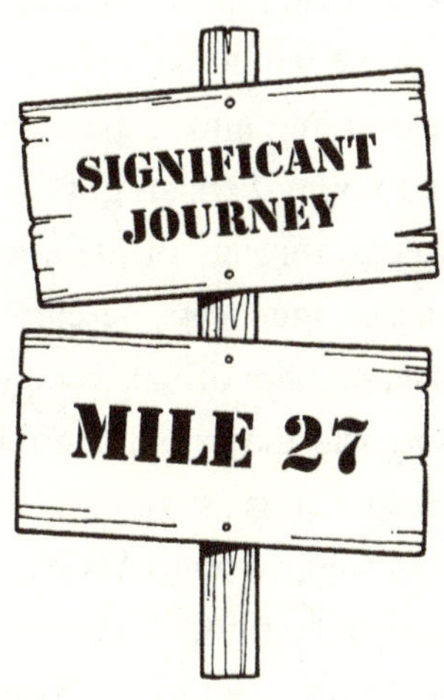

The sun was brilliant as we passed a volcano, 20,000-feet high, on the way to the Caspian Sea. The ski tow on its flank looked new. The road descended, following the edge of a churning river lined with evergreen trees. The wooden gabled houses gave this area more of a European look than Oriental.

We caught glimpses of women in bright printed dresses, rosy cheeks peeking out of white caps, and men wearing Russian-style fur hats. We were close to the Russian border. People we passed would wave, and others would surround us wherever we stopped. In one village we bought huge flat sheets of bread straight off the rope clothesline hanging over the sidewalk. It was tough but delicious with the jam we bought. And it was a nice break from our eggs, potatoes, and carrots—all things we could peel. The eggs were cheap there—75 cents for fifteen.

For the night, we pulled over in a place with a big sign that said "Wild Life Park." It wasn't much, but a creek ran alongside it. We built a big bonfire, and the next morning we washed our clothes and hair in the icy stream. The air had the feel of an early spring day, and there were some new buds on the bare tree branches. It was the perfect place to stop for a bit and thaw out, straighten out the van, and reorganize. The next day we would be arriving in the last large town in Iran, Mashad, before crossing into Afghanistan.

In Mashad we met a young Persian guy. We were walking down the street noticing the large throngs of men, many of them wearing turquoise turbans. I was intrigued by the carts on the street corners selling small various shaped bars of baked clay inscribed in Persian. Soon we found ourselves near the gate of a gold-domed mosque. Two turquoise-turbaned men spat at us as we passed by.

A young man in jeans stepped up to Alain and gently took his arm. In perfect American English he said, "Today is the anniversary of the prophet's death. You might not want to go closer to the mosque gate."

"Thanks! We didn't know," Alain replied.

"Mashad is the third holy city of the Muslims. Come with me. I can show you the city if you like."

His name was Ahmed, and the little clay tablets we saw for sale were called prayer stones, and they were used to place your forehead against when kneeling in prayer. The Peace Corps worker who had taught Ahmed English two years ago was from Iowa. He was friendly and told us all about his life in Mashad. He hoped to own his own carpet shop one day.

He took us to a restaurant and introduced us to the national dish called *abgosht*. Along the back of the stove in most cafes were many pint-sized metal pots with lids. For about 60 cents each, we were served a full pot, a metal bowl and pestle, a plate of flat bread, and a sliced sweet red onion.

In the pot was a stew of potatoes, lamb, tomatoes, white beans, saffron, and other seasonings, which had been simmering on low heat for about twelve hours. To properly eat this, we were to break some of our bread into bite-sized pieces into the bowl then cover it with juice from the stew and slices of onion. When our bowl was empty, we were to then place the potatoes, meat, and beans into the bowl and mash them with the pestle. This was then covered with sliced onions and dipped up with the remaining chunks of bread. All of this was washed down with very hot sweet tea.

The tea was served in small glasses with tiny spoons and miniature saucers similar to the ones in Turkey, except the glasses were a different shape and usually had designs on them.

We were so glad to know about *abgosht*. It was cheap, delicious, and hot. Later we learned that there were two prices for *abgosht*, the tourist price and the regular price. We never cheated a restaurant owner, but we learned to firmly set down the right coins for the regular price, smile, and walk out.

Our friend Ahmed also took us to an old camel "hotel" where we found a dozen smiling Mongol-featured boys working on torn carpets. The boys took the repaired carpets outside and stretched them out on the dirt roadway. They left them outside for a while, letting the traffic—cars, trucks, and horse-drawn carts—run over them. This was so the repaired sections would blend in to the rest of the carpet. Some of the small carpets were only twenty dollars, but that was still over our budgets.

I wanted to visit with the little "Eskimo" boys. They looked so familiar to me, as if they had just dropped in from Alaska where I grew up. In one room on the second floor were several shy girls sitting cross-legged in front of weaving frames making new carpets. They were weaving small pieces of colored wool yarn into intricate patterns. I watched for a while and wondered what the girls were thinking and talking about as they worked.

The camel building was two stories high and surrounded a large courtyard where camels were kept when a caravan stopped over night. The space was now used for businesses instead of a hotel. One of the businesses was a "spaghetti" factory. Two men were kneading and cutting dough into long thin strips on a wood plank table. They then hung the strips of dough over rope lines in the open air to dry before storing and selling the pasta. The old camel hotel had probably been there for hundreds, maybe thousands of years. Perhaps Marco Polo stopped here. It was right on his route—it was all so amazing to me!

Ahmed then took us to a turquoise factory. Several men and boys sat at little tables in a small room polishing the stones on lathe-type machines. They seemed very happy to have us visit them, and they willingly showed us all the steps in their work. I bought three polished chunks for one dollar.

At the end of the day, we bought some transmission fluid, motor oil, and a spark plug at a gas station. They gave us permission to park under their light overnight. A dog with six pups huddled in some rubble beside the station. The workers looked aghast when I picked up a pup and petted it. Ahmed explained that the men were amused that anyone would want to touch a dirty dog. The pups resembled Saint Bernard dogs. I wished I could feed and fatten up all the dogs and horses we had seen on this trip.

It was difficult to say good-bye to Ahmed. He had kept us safe and had been very helpful. We planned to write to him.

The next morning the gas station people woke us up at 6 a.m. It was still dark as we drove out of town and stopped to sleep a few more hours near a cluster of factory buildings. The countryside had turned dry and dusty. We had gotten our Afghani and Pakistani visas before we met our friend in Mashad. They were free and easy to get, and we didn't have to wait long, so we were ready to cross the border into Afghanistan.

What we thought would be an easy process took longer because we had to buy car insurance, go through customs, fill out forms on the cameras and our belongings, and then change money at the bank. Our car had to be searched. A young boy around 9 years old searched our car, and I wondered if he actually held this as an official position.

Darkness descended on us as we drove a long lonely stretch heading toward the first village, Herat, in Afghanistan. We were glad there was no traffic. It was pitch black and our headlights hardly pierced the night. It was too desolate to camp out there so we kept driving. Just five miles before Herat, the engine sputtered to a stop. We were out of gas, but we had more in our spare jug. The only trouble was our only source of light was candlelight, which of course we could not use. At least some of the fuel managed to end up in the tank because we made it to Herat.

We remembered the advice from the "Pudding Shop" in Istanbul to always park in hotel parking lots for safety while in Afghanistan. We were hungry and wouldn't be able to buy groceries till morning when the markets were open, so our plan was to find a hotel for parking and dinner.

The few buildings we passed on the streets of Herat were dark, even the one we saw with a hotel sign out front. It looked fancy on the outside with tall pillars and a broad stairway climbing to the oversized double doors that opened off the covered veranda. Inside we found ourselves standing in an empty and dimly lit hall that branched into a "T". Intricately-decorated carpets were layered two and three deep on the floor. A couple of men were leaning against the walls. A handful of women and children were squatting or sitting on the carpets in the dark halls.

Directly opposite the front entrance and through a set of glass paneled doors we could see a couple of small tables surrounded by wood chairs. On both sides of these doors were glass cabinets. Only one shelf was occupied, holding two cans, one with a picture of peas on it and another with a picture of some white vegetable.

A man hurried out from the dining room. Smiling, he gestured for us to come in. We sat down but soon realized we had no idea how to ask about the menu. Our helper realized the same thing, so he motioned for us to follow him. He took us to the display cabinet and showed us the dusty can of peas. The price he showed us on his fingers sounded atrocious, so we figured we had better skip the peas. Next we followed our host out the double doors down the hall to the right.

At the end of the hall, he pushed through a swinging metal door into a large empty room, empty except for the woman who sat in the middle of the floor with a kerosene cooker in front of her. It was just like ours. Beside her was a basket of eggs. Wrapped in a white frayed cloth at her knee was some flat bread. So the menu was eggs, bread, and tea. We could have them cook it for us or we could buy the food and cook it ourselves. We paid four Afghani each for two eggs. We then thanked the woman and took the eggs back to the van to cook. As it was, we were paying twenty Afghani each just to park in the parking lot overnight. The rates were per person, not car. So we couldn't afford to let the professional cook fix our meal.

We woke up to find ourselves immersed in the life of a much earlier century. We saw few signs of electricity. The wide concrete street in front of our hotel was lined with tamarack-like evergreen trees. The dusty road was filled with people on bikes and wagons pulled by horses and donkeys. The one-storied buildings along the sides were all connected with arched double door fronts with fancy details in the concrete trims. It was difficult to tell what kind of business was operating in the flat-topped, open-fronted shops.

Double wooden doors of different designs folded back to leave the fronts of these businesses open to the public. Most had signs above their doors indicating what type of business was inside, but we, of course, couldn't read them. Fortunately, an auto repair shop gave itself away by the Volkswagen emblem tied with a string above the opening. They were busy with bike repairs, but they made room for us and took the time to change the oil in our van.

Once in awhile we saw a man in western dress but most wore baggy cotton trousers and turbans. The women were covered from head to foot with long black shawls. In front of their eyes was a thinner mesh rectangle so that they could see. I caught glimpses of slim ankles sometimes and wondered how they survived the heat in the summer.

Stumbling into a good-sized bazaar, we bought a blue-enameled teapot for a few pennies. Even the metal household items were colorful and exotic. Young boys, faces round and cheeks rosy, hawked hand-knitted wool socks for 20 cents a pair. Two sidled up to us, shyly holding out their wares that were draped over their arms. I spied a red and black pair in the arms of the smallest boy and bought them. As soon as I paid him, he turned and hightailed it around the corner, the bigger boy sending him on his way with what sounded like expletives.

Carved chests and chairs were stacked with carpets and coats. The shops were filled with people bantering and bargaining. Once in awhile Alain heard a few words of French. We walked down a tree-lined street, passing carriages pulled by horses trimmed in red tassels and jingling bells.

As we drove on south, the country opened onto a broad plateau with rock-strewn mountains jutting straight up 20,000 feet or more above sea level out of the sand with no trees in sight. The roads were in good shape. Somewhere we had heard that they were built as a joint project between Russia and America years ago.

Tollgates every few miles blocked the highway. At the ones located near villages, people approached the few and far between vehicles to sell eggs, potatoes, carrots, and oranges. If it hadn't been for the armed men manning these gates, we wouldn't have taken the gates too seriously—the gates were just slender logs blocking the road that had to be lifted and moved by hand for each vehicle after the toll was collected. Next to each gate sat a pile of wrecked vehicles of all descriptions. We figured that was the result of what happened after dark, and we decided to never drive at night again.

Along the way we saw many *caravanserai*—these mud-walled compounds served as stopovers similar to the camel hotels in Iran. They were situated every few miles, a day's journey by camel. Some of them had latticed walls with turrets and towers on the corners. We saw no westerners, no one but the occasional Afghani man standing alone along the roadside. Once in a great while we passed a brightly decorated bus, bundles tied to the top, stopped by the side of the road surrounded by its passengers squatting in the dust.

A few hours down the road we noticed a moving string of dark objects shimmering on the horizon. The line merged at a point with the highway further ahead. As they drew closer we could pick out camels, top heavy with huge swaying bundles, donkeys, dogs, sheep, goats, swaggering men, white teeth flashing in tanned faces, daggers hanging from wide leather belts, strong women swinging along in rich red and purple embroidered skirts, and smudge-faced children, some in packs on the sides of the camels. The women's long braids hung free from tasseled headscarves. Pewter and silver jewelry jingled from ankles, necks, and arms.

We were reluctant to drive on after the last little boy crossed the roadway with his little flock of sheep, wondering if what we saw passing just fifteen feet in front of us was real. These were nomadic people returning north to summer pastures where they would feed their flocks.

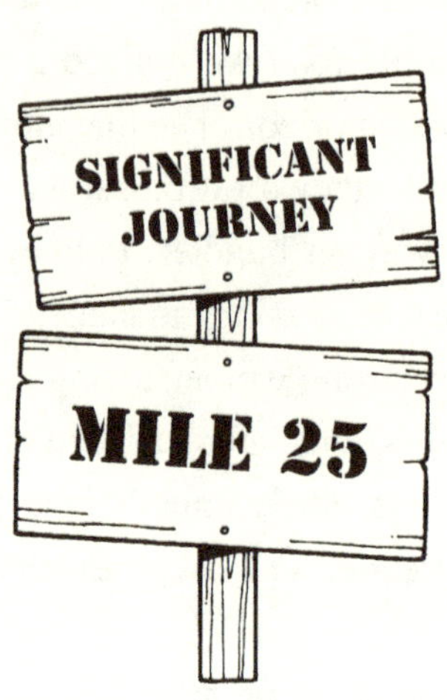

"Morning has become, Mister." The little man repeated this as he banged on our van. It was six in the morning and pitch-black still. We had pulled into a fenced compound near the village of Farah late the afternoon before and were granted permission to park. It was the only sign of civilization we had found anywhere on this stretch of desert country. The night watchman was waking us up. Perhaps he wanted us gone before the day crew came to work. The buildings looked as if they might belong to the highway maintenance department.

So we moved on and were in the bigger town of Kandahar before midday. We entered on the main street, which was lined with booth-like shops, many of them opening onto a platform built two feet or so above the sidewalk. We parked in front of a two-story building with a small sign labeled "Bank" at the end of the street, the tallest one around. It was closed, so we waited in the van until we saw someone enter.

Inside was a high-ceilinged vestibule lined with locked doors. Climbing a wide staircase to the second floor, we found two uniformed men standing on either side of the only open doorway. In the middle of this large vaulted room was another man sitting behind a metal desk.

No other furnishings or customers were present, just us, the man at the desk, and the guards. I half expected the banker to pull a shoebox full of cash out from under his chair, but he retrieved some Afghani money from a small closet at the back of the room in exchange for our American Express checks.

After our transaction was complete, we headed back to the van. We were not sure how safe our things would be, so we took turns staying with the van.

When Alain was taking his turn exploring and I was sitting in the van, two tall Afghani men in deep conversation, gowns and turban tails flowing, approached. Stealthily I snapped a photo. I didn't notice until months later when I got the film developed that the right jacket sleeve on one of the men hung loose, and he had no hand.

A concrete trough ran down the side of the main street next to me. It was about a foot deep and two feet wide, and it was full of garbage, but the water was moving. On the sidewalk under the building overhang was a barber. His clients sat cross-legged on the dusty sidewalk facing him. He dipped his blade into a tin can of water and drew it across his customer's cheeks. Then the client unwound his turban and the barber shaved his head. After each patron the barber would go to the edge of the gutter, dump out his tin of water, and dip it in to fill it again.

I then noticed that directly behind me was a man with a painted cabinet on wheels. I watched as he folded down a side door to form a tabletop, set out a row of little china dishes, and filled them with yogurt. After paying him a few coins, his customers would take the little bowls and spoons and then stand in the shade of the overhang to eat their yogurt. When they finished, the yogurt man gathered up the little dishes, squatted over the ditch, rinsed them out, and refilled them from the large bowl of yogurt he kept in the cabinet.

Atamamad became our little 14-year-old friend in Kandahar. He was the son of his dad's oldest of three wives. With three families, there were many children, and he only saw his dad periodically. The first day we drove into town, he stopped by with his goods for sale. His sleeves were stuffed with chunks of hashish wrapped in foil, waxed paper bags of marijuana, and opium. Under his soft grey shirtsleeve he wore a large man's silver watch and had shiny rings on several fingers. He could speak Farsi, some German, English, and French. He had learned these languages because of his outgoing approach and dealing with traveling kids.

When we first got to Kandahar, we found a hotel to park at with an enclosed courtyard. The building acted as a fence for the parking lot in the middle. Atamamad asked us where we were parked to camp, and when we told him, he became very agitated. He told us we had to move at once.

He asked, "Didn't you see French car?"

Yes, we had seen a car with French license plates.

"Those kids, they go with the hotel man to his home. He feeds them big dinner and shows kids hashish. They think the hotel man is nice host and they smoke a lot of hashish. The hotel man is expecting kids to buy big bunch of hashish at end of dinner and to pay for what they smoke. The kids think it is just a nice evening and they don't buy after all. Nobody sees them any more. Their car is there for one month already," Atamamad breathlessly exclaimed.

He then directed us to what was supposed to be the police station parking lot. We never found out if it really was, but there were guards, and we never did hear what happened to the French traveling kids.

"Good evening!" No matter the time of day, Atamamad shouted this greeting to us when he saw us. From the moment we met him, he became our sidekick friend, assisting us with translating, telling us what to buy, and instructing us as to where we needed to go.

"Atamamad, this is a photo of my dog back home. Do you know where in Kandahar there are any dogs like this?" We were lounging with Atamamad against the side of the van, parked on the main street. I was hoping that this was the day that I would get to see a real Afghan Hound.

"*Sagee tazi! Sagee tazi*!" he exclaimed and away he ran. Soon he was back, smiling and excitedly explaining that we needed to drive to the outskirts of town where there was a *sagee tazi*.

"*Sagee tazi*, you dog," he explained.

So into the van we climbed, he right up front next to the open window calling and waving to all his friends and acquaintances as we passed. Winding our way through a cluster of mud shanties, we stopped and were immediately surrounded by a clutch of several dozen children, the little girls with charcoal around their eyes and earrings in their ears. In spite of their shyness, they pressed in close, shadowing our every move. We didn't mind.

An older boy led us with our entourage between huts where under some brush and refuse we found a batch of pups, about the size of full-sized cats. As far as we could determine, they were about two months old. But these pups were much too stocky and thick boned to be Afghan Hound pups, although they did have the floppy ears. But the ears might have been too short. Their tails did curl over their backs the right way. I picked them up one by one and looked at them. Pups change so much as they grow, especially Afghan Hound pups. I just couldn't tell.

Confounded and amid all the clamor of the neighborhood, I asked Atamamad if I could see the mother dog. When she was brought up, I was disappointed. She was stout and stocky with a stubby muzzle, short tan hair, and small ears, a generic dog. She was not an Afghan Hound. All the way back to the car, Atamamad and the neighborhood tried to convince me that these were *sagee tazi*. I shook my head because I now realized *sagee tazi* just meant "dog." This was the first of several dog runs that Atamamad took us on. As I got better at them,

I realized that the dog owners were expecting me to buy a dog. I just wanted to look at an Afghan Hound.

One day a stooped, wrinkled woman, toothless and gray-haired, grasped my elbow and thrust her other hand under my nose, begging. It sounded like she was asking for "matches." Atamamad and I were sitting on the edge of his family's shirt and jacket shop booth, legs dangling over the sidewalk. He had his lunch of cold fried fish and flat bread, the stained cloth in which they were wrapped spread out in front of him on the ground. The flies were thick on his fish, but he seemed unaware.

He didn't hesitate to give her a piece of his lunch, and as she sidled away, he said to me, "See, that's a real antique lady."

"How old is she?" I inquired.

He called out to her and she answered him. "Forty-four," he told me. Forty-five was the average life span for an Afghani person.

A few weeks later when we returned through Kandahar we found Atamamad in his shop. He was all stuffed up and coughing. I asked to have a look at his throat, and he obliged me. His tonsils were red and swollen, and I could tell he had a fever. Then I saw three parallel cuts about two inches long and a half an inch apart on his neck under his left ear.

"What happened here?" I asked him as I pulled his collar down.

"This was for my sickness," he answered, pointing at his throat. "From the barber."

It was 1973, and I was looking at a young boy who had been bled as treatment for a throat infection! He agreed to go with me to the pharmacy where I bought him some vitamin C and some throat lozenges. He stood outside a few steps away as I went in to buy the items. The pharmacy was a suspicious place to most of the simple folks here. After I left, I had the feeling he wouldn't take the vitamins.

It was time to move on toward warmer weather. India was still our ultimate destination. We would be only a few miles from there once we reached Kabul, the capital of Afghanistan. Alain was driving as we approached Kabul. He didn't have an international driver's license, but we didn't think that should be an issue. Especially in Afghanistan we drove an hour sometimes before seeing another vehicle, and we had never seen a police officer. Although it was pretty cold out, it was peaceful, and we were making good time across the endless stretches of high desert plateaus following a line of rugged mountains, the Hindu Kush. Opposite, on our right, not far away, was the Pakistani border.

Suddenly the air was filled with the wail of a siren. Five seconds later a black and chrome motorcycle nudged us to the rocky shoulder where a smartly uniformed police officer wearing knee-high polished black boots was soon writing us a ticket for speeding! We hadn't seen a village for miles. Nor had we ever seen a speed limit sign posted since entering the country. It was five dollars for speeding, and oh yes, another five dollars for Alain driving without an international driver's license. Of course, it was due and payable that instant.

A speeding ticket for a van that had to be manually pushed up most inclines more than two percent? A speeding ticket for a van that dropped ten miles per hour with each extra person it carried? A speeding ticket! And a fine of ten dollars! On five dollars a day we either put gas in the car or ate.

Tears came to my eyes. At that moment I missed home where we knew the rules and what to expect, and with two days of sustenance about to be stolen from us for a bogus accusation, I turned my face into my sleeve. Without warning, I was sobbing out my frustrations—the cold, the dry air, the toll gates, and my homesickness for home, which was half a world away.

There was a moment of awkward silence as I wiped my nose. Suddenly, without a word, the officer took the ticket out of Alain's hand and motioned for us to follow him up a narrow dirt track to a small stout stone building that blended into the surrounding boulders. He led us on his spiffy motorcycle. We parked next to a big rock, and a little shakily, followed him into the small garden shed-sized hut.

It was then that he turned, smiled, and, making a grand gesture, pulled the ticket out of his pocket and ripped it into pieces. Then he poured us cups of tea and offered us beautiful oranges out of a basket on his desk.

This was a country where barbers treated illnesses on the sidewalks and the yogurt man washed his cups in the ditch, where they might cut off your hand if you were caught stealing and a woman could be stoned for adultery. But it was also a country where we met a police officer with a soft and understanding heart.

We drove into Kabul and found the streets clogged with pedestrians, mainly men, with a small number of vehicles mixed in. A sprinkling of women were out shopping in their black *chadors* draped down to their ankles. I smiled and nodded when I passed them, all the while wondering about their lives. The main streets wound along the river running through the city center. Concrete buildings and lean-to shops lined the potholed roads. Wooden platforms the size and shape of bed frames were stacked up outside the tea shops, their woven rope seats graying in the rain and snow. Men sat together cross-legged on these platform couches in good weather, talking as they drank their tea. The most noticeable thing was that we were not under curious scrutiny as we were in Jordan and Turkey. Here we were pretty much treated as invisible.

The hotel compound where we parked to camp was quiet. We were the only ones there. Because it was so cold, we inquired about getting rooms in the hotel, thinking we would be warmer, but we were informed that the rooms are unheated, and we would have to buy our own fuel to heat them! It was cheaper to just pay for parking and stay in the van.

The tourist office was well organized and the people were helpful. It was nice and warm there, and we would have stayed longer, but it was obvious that we were just killing time. We did buy two books, one in English and one in French, about Afghanistan. It took us most of a day to get our visas stamped, to find the bazaar, and to pick up some groceries. It was tempting to eat from the roadside food stands, but we stuck to our main menu of peeled items—eggs, potatoes, onions, and carrots.

It took sixty-eight Afghanis to equal one American dollar. Eggs were a better price the further we drove into Afghanistan, only one and a half Afghani each. Piles of oranges glowed golden in the drab winter markets. We bought two kilos of oranges for twenty Afghanis. They were delicious. Potatoes were ten Afghani for one kilo and onions were six. Huge raised glazed doughnuts were four Afghanis. A western loaf of bread was twenty Afghanis. We bought a whole meal at a three-star hotel for fifty cents per person. Not only was the food a feast but it was a bargain. We also filled up our drinking water tank at the hotel thanks to an outdoor spigot. The French-speaking hotel desk clerk reassured us that the water was potable.

We couldn't help but notice the many European traveling kids with red glassy eyes and scanty threadbare clothing hanging on their bony frames, lounging in doorways against buildings. They were adrift in a foreign land, dependent on opium or hashish. For most of them, their money was gone, and they had no way to get home. A big sign at the border forbid hashish and marijuana from either coming in or going out of the country, but we knew from talking to traveling kids in Istanbul that one of the main goals of most kids coming to Afghanistan was to get these drugs. We also knew that many ended up in jail. Near a bakery I met a tired looking girl whose boyfriend had been in prison for six years on a drug charge. She was from Connecticut and had been working with officials to get him released.

The bazaar was full of dresses, shirts, and purses, many of them made out of previously used articles of clothing. I found an intricately stitched fabric bag, a pair of embroidered leather boots, and a burgundy colored Kushi tribal dress all for two dollars. It didn't matter to me that the cuffs and hem of the dress were frayed from previous wear.

As we wandered the streets, we often heard flute music. We never saw anyone playing the flute, but we heard it. The men in the shops seemed sober and hard-working. It was hard to imagine any of them playing flutes. Rambling down dark damp streets and wide but empty out of the way boulevards, we came across a sign in English advertising a perfume factory. It was a little hole in the wall, and the perfumes were displayed in tiny jars and screw-top bottles with names typed on strips of notebook paper and taped on with scotch tape. For 10 cents I picked out a small vial of "Rose."

The ground was frozen, and there was snow on the ground. The cold permeated everything. My hands hadn't been warm for weeks. The shop stalls were tiny and there was no space to warm up. We were too conspicuous to just sit in the few hotel lobbies, and we couldn't afford to go to restaurants. The only heat we had in the van was the kerosene cook stove we had bought in Istanbul. It had taken the place of the backpack propane stove we could only use in Europe where that fuel was available.

Our kerosene stove was about twelve inches high with room for one pot on top—it was the same as what we saw used all through the Middle East. The fuel tank formed the base. To light the stove, we had to first pump it to build up air pressure in the fuel tank. There was a small doughnut shaped bowl, which we called the pre-burner, circling the fuel outlet. We filled this with alcohol and lit it with a match while slowly opening the fuel valve. The fire then lit the fuel. We never lit the stove unless a window was open.

Although it was only five o'clock in the afternoon, it was already dark. Perched on the end of the plywood platform in the back of the van, I was peeling some carrots and potatoes to fry with scrambled eggs. Then I made what we called apple pie. I sautéed rolled oats with a little olive oil, brown sugar, and cinnamon. I then divided it into two bowls. Next I sautéed chopped apples until they were soft, and then pouring them over the oats. It was amazing what we could do with only one frying pan. Alain reclined behind me reading. The middle windows were open on both sides of the van between us.

Suddenly my head was gripped by a tremendous pounding pain. Dizzily I tried to speak, but my vision and hearing began to fade into darkness. All I could do was mumble, "Alain, the door! I can't see!"

He flung it open and urged me to fill my lungs with fresh air. It was a struggle to sit up and stay awake. Everything was black, muffled, and far away.

"I'm OK, I'm OK," I repeated over and over, fighting off the dizzy blackness.

We knew right away that it had to be the stove putting out carbon monoxide. Alain was OK because he had been closer to the windows.

I was sitting directly over the stove.

Legs wobbly and head pounding, I stumbled through the muddy streets for the next three hours leaning on Alain's arm, hoping that the walking would clear my system. The excruciating headache didn't leave me until the next day.

Later when we were back home, I described the symptoms to my doctor, and he told me I was very fortunate. The reason why people who die from carbon monoxide poisoning are often found sitting at a table as if nothing was wrong is because there are no warning symptoms until the blood level has reached the level to cause death. The only thing we did wrong was to exercise because this spread the carbon monoxide throughout my whole system, but we were right about getting out in the air immediately. My doctor then added, "Someone was watching out for you that day!"

The mountains towered around us in Kabul, beautiful with newly fallen snow, but they held hostage the frigid air. I was huddled under a blanket in the van reading when I heard a dog bark, a bark that sounded just like an Afghan Hound! Pulling back the curtains, my eyes fell on a fine-boned cream-colored dog, tail curled over her back, ribbons of silky hair edging her chest and legs. Her coat was not as thick and long and she was smaller, but she had the unmistaken build of an Afghan Hound. I jumped out of the van and stretched my hand toward her. Her tail wagged and she moved closer to me.

She was wandering around in the hotel compound. They told me that I could buy her for forty dollars. She could be my *sagee tazi*! I was very tempted, but the endless borders yet to cross and the import papers needed to take her to America were small obstacles compared to living in a small van with a big dog for the next few months. I knew taking her home was impossible. But seeing her made me homesick, really homesick.

We had been on the road close to ten months. Saturated with

strangeness and stressed with unfamiliarity, we spent much of our time talking about hot water out of a faucet, electric lights to read by, lettuce in a salad, and soft toilet paper. We dreamed of building barns, raising chickens, baking bread, having a refrigerator.

We decided to not go any further east. The strain of the cold, the snow ahead on Khyber Pass, and our need of new tires kept us from relishing any thoughts of going to India. Regardless of the expense and effort we went through to get the precious insurance documents for that country and in spite of the promise of warmer weather a day's journey away, the adventure of travel no longer had as much appeal as heading home. We turned around in Kabul. Anything further east would remain unexplored by us. We knew the way back home, fourteen time zones back. This was the day to head west.

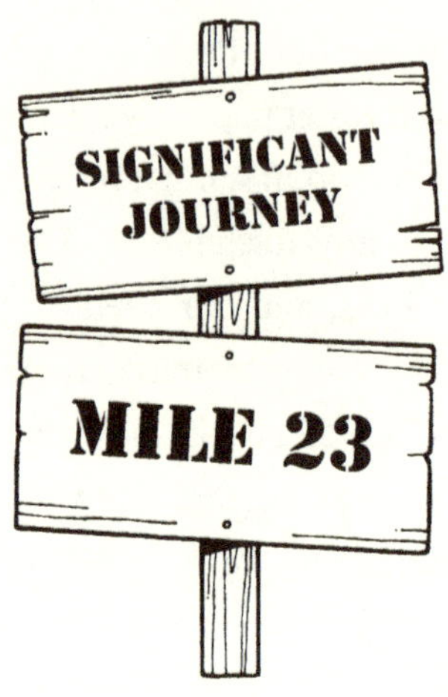

It was spring. But it wasn't obvious as yet there in Kabul, which is 6,000 feet above sea level. We wanted to see some spring. A big load was lifted off our shoulders after we made the decision to turn around. Someday we could come back, but that day we were headed home!

Ghazni was a smaller village at a little lower altitude. We felt like we were on holiday, and the parking at the hotel was free. We never did figure out why we had been charged per person at the other hotels when it was the car that was parking. We found some brass camel bells for seventy cents to take back for my horse.

The next morning the sun glistened off the tin roof of the gas station outside a small village called Mogul. We pulled into the inside pump. Alain jumped out and uncorked the gas tank. The attendant was already halfway across the dusty lot from his shady spot beside the mud daubed hut. Grey robes swishing around his knees, the weight of the buckle pulled his leather girdle down on the right side. His turban tail fell over one ear as he gave me a swarthy glance. I smiled but remembered that he deeply disapproved of me, a woman with an uncovered face. I liked his leather boots.

Our tank was not empty, but we knew that we needed just about thirty liters of petrol. The capacity of the tank was forty liters. The gas gauge had never worked, but we kept good records of our miles on our trusty notepad taped to the steering column. When we had gone close to two hundred miles, we filled the tank up. Two times too many, we had run out of fuel driving more than that. This time we had driven one hundred and fifty three miles since last topping off the tank.

Weeks before, at the Afghanistan border crossing, we had twisted our way through a handful of nondescript cement buildings to find the one with the currency exchange sign. Startling rich red velvet draperies hung from ceiling to floor across the middle of the small room we had entered. A clean-cut man in a western-style blue gabardine suit had sat quietly at a metal desk behind the drapes.

"How much money would you like to exchange," he had asked in excellent English as he motioned for us to sit in the folding chairs facing him.

"Twenty-five dollars for now," Alain had replied, taking out some American Express checks and signing them. We didn't know it then, but this man would be the only western-dressed man we would see for quite awhile.

"How far is it to the next gas station," I had wanted to know.

"You won't find one until Herat, but it will be helpful for you to know that the petrol has a set government price of six Afghani per liter. Sometimes a gas station attendant may try to get you to pay more. But tell him that you know the government price."

We really appreciated this man's interest in us.

"Oh, and keep your eye on the pump. Some don't have a glass covering and the attendant may attempt to manually move the needle on the gauge to bring a higher total while the tank is filling."

This man was the first person to see us for what we were, not rich westerners, just travelers interested in seeing what his country was like. His obvious warmth and helpfulness almost brought tears to my eyes. Instead, we both smiled and shook his hand, reluctant to leave his red curtained cozy corner and re-enter the world outside where we were forever on guard.

Back in Mogul, the attendant handed Alain the pump handle and positioned himself to block my view of the pump gauge. I should have gotten out and stood where I could see if he moved the needle. Now he was standing in my way, and I would bump into him if I opened my door.

In a few minutes the pump clicked off. The tank was full. The attendant pointed to the gauge. The numbers were in Persian so they were meaningless to us. I held up both hands twice, indicating I was paying him for a full tank, two-hundred and forty Afghani, which I then placed in his outstretched palm. I knew that I was not short-changing him as I started to roll up the window. In fact, I was paying him more than I owed him. Alain had already started the van.

Immediately the attendant was next to me, gesturing at the money in his hand. Did I give him a wrong bill? I took the money back, counted it carefully in his view, and, with a nod and a smile, handed it back. But he waved his arms and began to shout. I took a piece of paper and wrote on it "240," then pointing to the tank, I wrote "40." He shook his head. Pointing at the tank, he grabbed the pencil out of my hand and made angry slashes showing 65! He was saying that we had put in sixty-five liters into a tank that held around forty liters! Just then a taxi drove up, and we engaged the driver in the discussion. After five minutes of arguing, it was no use. The taxi drove off. By now the attendant was at Alain's side of the van, motioning for him to follow him into the mud hut.

"Alain, don't go! What can he show you there that he can't show you here? This seems suspicious!" I spoke hurriedly.

"OK, then let's just leave. We didn't cheat him." With that, Alain closed his door and started to pull away, but a rough hand grasped the window ledge. It startled us and for a moment we just sat, motor idling.

"Let me trade places with you. He won't touch a female, so I can drive on out," I said, sliding into the driver's seat. As Alain got out of the car to come around to the passenger's side, the attendant thought Alain was going over to the hut with him, so he let go of the car. Quickly, as Alain slid into place, I put the car into gear. Suddenly the brawny arm of the attendant made a lunge and grasped the steering wheel! At the same time, his free hand reached inside his robe and emerged with a small dagger about eight inches long. The blade was covered with a leather sheath. Between shaking it under my nose, he attempted to brush off the cover. So much for expecting him to be more cooperative around a woman!

No longer was I polite. I opened my mouth and yelled directly into his face, tightening my double grip on the steering wheel. Alain was shouting in French. The turbaned attendant was lividly screaming in Farsi. Another robed and turbaned Afghani trotted out of the hut. At this moment it wasn't the money as much as it was the principle. Well, it was the money, too!

I saw the stocky wrist and hand six inches in front of my nose. The next instant my teeth chomped down hard on the meaty base of his thumb. I didn't know I was going to do that! It surprised even me, but it was a good move because at the same moment Alain surprised himself and threw a strong right hook straight into the attendant's chin.

Suddenly the car was free. I shoved the gas peddle to the floor and that old '58 Volkswagen van smoked out of the lot and up onto the highway. The door swung shut with a crash and the window crumbled into tiny glass cubes inside the door. We didn't breath, slow down, or speak for a good half hour. Finally, it was with huge sighs of relief that we turned and grinned at each other. We were out of danger, and we were doing OK. In fact, we were doing just fine! It was then we knew that no one would ever find us on any “Missing Person” poster in any embassy! We stopped and danced a jig on the side of that lonely road.

On our exit from Afghanistan, we each were handed a small paper cup full of antibiotic capsules and told to take them all at once. There had been a cholera outbreak, and Iran didn't want any untreated people entering their country. We had had our cholera shots in Istanbul, but that didn't matter. Because we refused to take the pills all at once, we were detained at the border for awhile, but they finally agreed to let us take the capsules over a period of a few days.

We were in good spirits and were excited to be heading home. Stopping not far into Iran, we camped at a bubbling brook. The water was clear and cold, but we washed our hair and clothes, draping them over the bushes to dry in the thin spring sun. All day long we were a roadside attraction with groups of people stopping and watching us. Several spread blankets and ate picnic lunches. The altitude was so much lower than in Afghanistan, and the air was nice and soft.

Near the Caspian Sea, we parked and hiked across a number of fenced fields to take photos and put our hands in the water so that we could say we had touched the Caspian Sea. I saw men wearing beige knitted caps with earflaps, unique for this area. In a café in the village Kord, I asked where I could buy one, and before I knew it, a man walked in and offered me the one off his head. They were made out of camel wool.

Almost every village in Iran had a circle roundabout with a huge monument of some sort all lit up with colored lights. In Tehran these traffic circles were even grander. There we went to the huge market and found the bowls, mashers, and small kettles to make *abgosht*. We then went to a café to get an *abgosht* meal. But we were disappointed when we were handed a bowl of clear broth with no bread, onions, or our own little pot of stewed garbanzos and lamb. Asking to see where the broth originated, the cook led us into the kitchen and showed us the pot. In it was a calf's head, eyelashes, snout, whiskers, and all. We left without finishing our soup.

By now newborn lambs had joined the flocks across the northern plateau of Iran. We saw one shepherd stretched out on the new green, sleeping while his sheep nibbled grass around him. Another shepherd had hung his sheepskin coat on his staff like a scarecrow and stuck it in the ground. His sheep quietly ate around the "shepherd," while he was down the road a ways visiting with another shepherd. Most of the shepherds wore big round fur caps. As we passed many of the shepherds, we at first thought they were blowing us kisses. But we finally figured out they were asking us for cigarettes.

We camped in the city of Tabriz. The next day we planned to cross the border into Turkey. We hoped the spring weather held.

It was mid-afternoon already. The frantic rain and fierce fog declared that the day would be as frozen as my feet. I couldn't focus on the chess game. It was Alain's move anyway. He balanced the game board on the box that served as our table. While he contemplated his next move, I took off my boots and layered on another pair of socks.

From where we were parked, we could not see the ribbon of road, raveled and without a shoulder, meandering across the high plateau to the west. Mountains marked our map ahead of us, heaps and heaps of them. I was anxious to be on the move, but the wind was too strong. We had to wait for the weather to clear before picking our way up the steep slopes ahead.

Dim and dark, the murky March sky outside did nothing to lift my spirits. Ahead of us was home, yet it was still more than 15,000 miles away. I peered out between the curtains. Several Turkish border patrol officers were huddled under an overhang on the lee side of their concrete office smoking. A dozen smashed cars rusted against the wire fence. One was a Volkswagen van like ours.

Did it belong to traveling kids like us? Run off the road by a truck? Maybe it hit the toll gate in the dark? Did the occupants survive? Were the travelers in any of the photos posted in the embassies: "Missing, our daughter, our son: Last in contact with us from Amman/Baghdad/Tehran. If anyone has information, please contact us in London/Los Angeles/Toronto. . ."

We had waited almost four hours for the wind to die down, and now the daylight was fading fast. I pulled back the curtains to check on the weather. The rain had stopped and the fog had lifted. My eyes trailed across the brassy fields of a wide valley and then stopped short. A cone-shaped, snow-covered mountain rose steeply up from the valley. With no foothills, it ascended straight out of the valley floor. Could this be Mount Ararat?

It was! One of the border guards confirmed it for me. Rummaging under the seat, I pulled out the little gift Bible from my parents. This was the first time I had opened it on this trip. I shuffled through its pages, found the story of Noah, and read it out loud to Alain. He had never heard that story before.

This day it was more than a story to me. It was real and we were here. I stood outside, no longer feeling the cold, just gazing at the mountain. To the west, east, and north were smaller mountain peaks as far as the eye could see, but to the southeast was a valley opening down toward Iraq and Jordan. It all made sense. That was where Noah would have found the best route out of these mountains. And he would have ended up in the Euphrates River valley. He was going where God wanted him to go. Was I?

The next morning we woke up to the van covered in a foot of heavy wet snow. It had been so late the day before when we left the border that we had only driven to the little village a couple of miles away. Two women in black boots, one carrying a bucket on her head, slogged past, lifting flowered skirt hems as they broke a trail to a small cottage. Freezing wind buffeted the van. We took no time to eat or to roll up our sleeping bags. Our first and only thought was to follow that ribbon of road up and over the mountains. We didn't need to hear the weather report. More snow was ready to fall out of the pile of low grey clouds off to the north.

Truck tracks marked our way, icy and sharply rising. The switchback turns became shorter and steeper. Hugging the mountainsides, we peered down on the tops of vehicles following behind us. Grinding onward up in second gear, we rounded a corner only to find our way blocked by a jackknifed tractor trailer. Another, carrying sheep, was on the upper side in the ditch. Other vehicles were stalled helter-skelter in our path. Alain didn't need to put on the brakes. We came to a complete stop and then slowly slid backward, defeated, into a snow bank.

An hour or so later we were back in the village below where we recognized and flagged down the car of some traveling kids we had met earlier in Iran. They were heading back up the mountain pass with tire chains and told us where to buy them. We hadn't eaten yet, and we were starving, so we decided to eat first. Snowdrifts left no place to pull off on the shoulder, but there was a cleared parking area next to a group of cement buildings. A man was walking near them . He nodded, which we interpreted as yes, to our hand motion inquiry about parking there.

What a relief to throw off boots and coats and stoke up the kerosene cooker. Soon I had onions, carrots, and potatoes simmering in a bit of olive oil, incidentally poured from our big gallon can that we bought in a shop somewhere on our trip. On its front it said, "Gift of the United States of America. Not to be bought or sold."

Startled by someone beating on the side doors of our van, I pulled the curtains open and found myself staring into the eyes of two very young gun-toting Turkish soldiers gesturing and urgently demanding us to move on. Why? We had no idea. We were parked in the only spot in the whole village that wasn't covered in snow. Although tired and hungry, Alain slipped on his boots, flung open the side door, moved a gun barrel out of his path on his way around to the driver's seat, climbed in, and fired up the ignition. As we rattled out of the parking lot, I balanced the cooking pots and juggled the potatoes on my lap. It was then that I heard a loud pop behind us! Turning, I saw a jeep with a soldier leaning out the window waving a gun in the air.

"That guy is shooting at us!" I cried. Just then I heard a second shot.

Alain slammed on the brakes. In an instant we were surrounded by jeeps. The soldiers jumped out and bodily yanked us from the van. I was in my stocking feet in the ice and mud. Soldiers were tearing through our belongings, tossing our things onto the side of the road. I in English and Alain in French were asking, "What is going on? What do you want?"

But our questions were ignored. Finally, above the confusion and chaos, I tearfully yelled one last desperate question, "Does anyone speak English?"

Unexpectedly, behind me I heard, "Hello, how are you?" Turning, I found a young soldier smiling broadly. Frantically, I grasped him by the sleeve.

"Oh thank goodness you speak English! Please tell us what is happening? What do they want? What is going on?"

"Today the sun is shining!" He smiled a pleased smile, and my heart fell to the bottom of my frozen feet. Turning away to hide my tears, in dismay I heard him repeat, "Hello, how are you?" Alain was as white as a sheet. We didn't need a weather report to tell us that no sun would be shining on us today.

Abruptly, the milling soldiers tossed our things back into the van, grabbed us both, stuffed us back into our van, and with a jeep in front and several behind, led us a short distance down the road to another cement building. We were directed into the parking lot full of deep snow, obviously to immobilize us. Several soldiers got out of their jeeps and pushed us in the last few feet.

Boots half on and laces dragging, we were then hustled up a broad stairway, through a set of double doors and down a long hall where our whole entourage burst into a small room. A dignified man in a dark suit and tie sat behind a wide wooden desk with his back to a window. Six men of various ages sat on folding chairs along the wall to his right. A rumpled old man stood, head down with cap in hand, facing the man behind the desk.

Our group jostled into the room, propelling us forward to face the man at the desk. By this time I had wiped the tears from my eyes, and wanting to be heard—to know what it was that we had done wrong and to find out what was going to happen—I shouted above the babble, "I want to know what is going on!"

All quieted, and then we heard, in perfect American English, "Perhaps I can help you." On jury duty and rising from one of the folding chairs, this Turkish man, who we later learned had graduated from dental school in Michigan, became our translator. The present trial was temporarily suspended while our hearing commenced. The old man whose trial we had interrupted had been given a seat.

Alain and I were exhausted. But we had to stand while the soldiers, guns hanging from straps on their shoulders, went through their stories. We then told our story through our new friend—how we couldn't make it up the mountain road, how we had looked for a place to park to eat our lunch, how we were then told to move on, and then when we were driving away, how we had been fired upon. The judge listened impassively, and then with an abrupt wave of his hand, he dismissed all of us. We were to return the next day, the dentist explained.

Back outside in the van we sat side by side—numb not only from what was happening but from the frost slowly creeping up the van sides. Dazed and despondent, we sat wrapped in all of our coats and blankets. We said little, but occasionally we pulled aside the curtains to glance at the three soldiers stationed around our van. Outside in the bitter cold, they swung their arms around and rubbed their shoulders to keep warm. As the hour grew late, the temperature continued to drop. We had forgotten our lunch, which had been handled and jostled about in the afternoon ransacking, but neither of us felt like eating anyway.

It seemed so long ago that we were sitting on a sunny beach on Crete with some other travelers. We had all heard of the recent conviction on drug smuggling charges of an American kid who was presently in jail somewhere in Turkey, and the rumors around his treatment in captivity were rampant. Descriptions of Turkish prisons kept twisting through my thoughts. What were they going to do to us?

The next morning I realized that our potatoes had disappeared. I had to go to the market to get some food. They let me go, but Alain was not permitted to leave. Even if they would've let him go, he was in no condition to be outside. He had woken up with an extremely sore throat and swollen tonsils. He was miserable, so he stayed curled up in his sleeping bag. I supposed he was considered the hostage to ensure my return.

Our joints were stiff, hands and feet chilled to the bone. Our drinking water was frozen solid in the jug. It was so cold even the Styrofoam ceiling of the van was frosted over.

Morning dragged into afternoon. How long would we be here? The whole thing with the judge was overwhelming enough. Now Alain was sick. No one had come to tell us what the plan was. We were sitting there packed into the snow like a homemade ice cream tub. I had to get the snow away from the walls of the van so that we could warm up. I scratched a circle through the icy window and saw that the soldiers were still guarding us.

Kicking open the doors, I jumped out into the snow. Startled, the soldiers came to attention—all eyes glued on me. Making the motion of throwing snow over my shoulder, I asked one of the soldiers for a shovel, but I got no response. I tried with the next soldier but again no response, not even a nod of the head. So I began to dig out the snow with my mittened hand, as futile as this was.

A third try with much more exasperation than charm, I spoke in a loud clear voice directly into the nearest face, "Please may I have a shovel?" The only response was a few amused mumbles. For the last time, louder, "We are freezing! I need to get the snow away from the van. Could you get me a shovel?" That time there was an exchange of smirks.

I then knew what I should do. With renewed determination, I marched up the steps, strode down the hall, and burst into yesterday's little room. The folding chairs, now empty, lined the wall. The same judge, alone and very astonished, sat at the big desk. I slumped down into the closest chair and blurted out through threatening tears, "We are freezing, and I need a shovel to move some snow away from the car. And I want to know why we are waiting! I would just like to go home!" My voice wavered, and I turned to hide my tears.

When I looked up, our Turkish dentist friend was beside me. He walked back to the van with me, examined Alain, and brought him some medications. He then spoke to the soldiers, and one of them brought me a shovel. As our dentist friend left, he informed us that we would have a hearing before the day ended.

The soldiers gathered close and watched me shovel. Naturally, none volunteered to help. I continued to dig, clearing a good section. It felt good to be doing something. My anger and frustration at the injustice of it all gave me more energy. I tried not to fling too much snow toward the stalwart guards. Stopping for a moment to check on Alain, I leaned my shovel against the side of the van. When I came back, my shovel was gone! I guess I was making too much progress.

It was almost dusk when the soldiers escorted us back to the judge's chambers. He had made a decision. Our crime was that we parked in a military compound yesterday to eat our lunch, and since he was a civilian judge, he was handing us over to a military judge who was headquartered in the next village to the east. What had confused the issue further was the red contact paper stars mixed in with the red contact paper maple leaves we had used for decoration on our van. The Russians use red stars as emblems in their country, and there hadn't always been peace between them and Turkey. Plus it hadn't helped that we were in the middle of Kurdish territory in Turkey where there was a lot of tension already. He handed us a sheaf of papers, and we all stumbled out.

It took five soldiers to push our car out of the snowdrifts. One rode beside me on the passenger side and a stuffed-full jeep followed behind us. On the way to the military judge, we passed a shepherd boy idling away his time with his sheep near the side of the road. We had learned at the "Pudding Shop" in Istanbul that shepherds would sometimes throw clods of dirt at windshields of travelers' cars, and it had been that way all through Turkey. So we didn't think anything about it when the clod hit our windshield. But the Turkish soldier was startled and shouted, "Halt! Halt!"

Alain slammed on the brakes. The soldier leapt out of the van and directed the jeep behind us to pull over. As one man, the jeep emptied, and they all ran back to the surprised and shocked shepherd boy, pitched him down, and pummeled him into the prairie stubble. We sat there speechless. As we got back on the road, we were glad to see the shepherd stand and wobble over to his flock. I was pretty sure he would never lob another clod again!

At the military headquarters, it took less than five minutes for the polished commander to read our report, stamp it, turn to us, and say, "I apologize for this incident. You're free to go!" It took us another five minutes to drink the hot chocolate he served us, but only because it was piping hot. Later we didn't wonder, we knew that Someone was watching out for us.

It was all over. Well, almost. We still had to cross the icy, slippery mountains.

The following morning the sky was blue and clear. We bought a pair of snow chains, headed back up the mountains, found the chains too big, returned them for the right size, and finally by late afternoon, made it over the icy pass. The air temperature was well below zero by then, and the snow and ice had built up and frozen in the wheel wells making it impossible to turn the tires more than a few inches left or right. We were glad that the road had straightened. The whole underside of the van was packed six inches thick with snow and ice. We couldn't shift. Nothing worked properly in the cold, so we drove in second gear.

We kept driving, hoping to drop altitude and warm up, but it didn't happen all day. At night the temperature plunged lower. At a small village, a kind hotel man let us stay at no cost and fed us a supper of stew and bread. The room was not heated, but it was warmer than the car

The van had a flat tire in the morning. The car was slowly disintegrating. With the spare on, we hobbled into the next town, Ezancum, where we bumped into some British kids we had met back in Afghanistan. They told us about a gas station with a spray hose we could use to get the ice off our car. They had a little black pup with them, a *sagee tazi.*

On our way again, by afternoon we were at lower altitudes, passing through newly plowed spring fields and admiring countless new lambs and blossoming fruit trees. The red roofs, the painted wagons, even the mud puddles, helped to our raise our spirits. The air was soft, and we felt carefree as we crossed the bridge into Istanbul. Here our car was put back together, the broken window, the speedometer, the tire, even the horn got fixed. A few days later as we left for Central Europe we knew we were on the homestretch.

Apparently it was not a good thing to have Afghanistan stamped on our passports. No one spoke English at the Bulgarian border crossing, but it was obvious from the reaction of the heavyset border guard perusing our passports that this was the case. Pounding his billy club to emphasize his words, he demanded we pull out the whole contents of our van and pile it on a long metal table under an overhang. Then we watched as he and his partner minutely and methodically examined each item. Our food, our clothes, our boxes, even our spices were opened and discussed. The jar of oregano was rushed into the building, but it was returned thirty minutes later by a sheepish sentry trying to appear nonchalant. Two weary hours went by. Other cars passed through with little trouble. The "bulldog," as we named him, finally called it quits, and with a last swing of his billy club, he ordered us to put our stuff back. He then returned our passports and reluctantly waved us on.

Yugoslavia was more welcoming. We found a shop where we got the oil changed in the van and savored some delicious bread and cheese. Then, after a few hours in Italy sauntering around Venice, we headed over Brenner Pass into Austria and then Germany.

In Germany it was a different story. There they took one look at the stamps on our passports and brought out two German shepherd dogs to sniff out the car. It didn't matter that it was raining and their eight feet muddied up our things. The officials checked the car carefully, even pulling the panels off the inside of the doors and examining the tires. Once again our spices and herbs were checked out, but this time it was the sage that got tested.

Fortunately, they too let us pass after their thorough inspection. After Germany we headed to France, and more specifically Paris. It was spring and the daffodils were blooming in the parks. We moseyed along the walkway above the Seine River, ate baguettes with Brie cheese, bought big doughnuts in the Latin Quarter, and sat on the grass under the Eiffel Tower. In fact, we camped under it for four days until authorities politely asked us to park elsewhere.

No longer did we need to hire guards to keep us safe. We were no longer held prisoner. We no longer had to deal with knives being pulled on us or guns being shot at us. We could use our regular camping stove and fuel again, which was a good thing because a part of the kerosene burner fell into the river when I was cleaning it.

Life was good on the Seine River. We decided to stay for awhile, so we found a nice parking lot on the seawall. The bistro owner who managed the lot looked the other way, and we showed our appreciation by keeping a low profile while his patrons came and went. It was the perfect place to sit and watch the boats go by. The Eiffel tower was just across from us. At night its peach tinted lights reflected off the indigo river while the waves lapped at our feet and soft music drifted lazily from the bistro. We talked about the future—our future. We planned to meet in the Pacific Northwest and spend the rest of our lives together. This was a big decision, but it hadn't taken us long to decide because we truly loved each other.

Meanwhile, Alain was out of funds, so he was flying home to Quebec the next day, back to his job. For now, we said good-bye. April in Paris was no longer appealing to me, so after dropping him off at the airport, I headed south.

It was still spring, and I didn't need to head home to my job as a school nurse until the fall. Traveling had lost some of its luster with Alain gone, but I decided I should just as well take advantage of having a place to stay and places yet to see in Europe. Parking in a village on the Spanish Riviera, I got some sun while sorting and labeling the photos from our journey. I then meandered west through northern Spain, passing through Barcelona, Pamplona, and San Sebastian.

One day, out of curiosity, I stopped and looked more closely at one of the many little roadside shrines. Very little traffic interrupted me on the quiet Spanish country road, so I took my time examining it. This particular one was built like a little cathedral with red silk poppies woven around the edges of the open front. Several used candles sat on the little floor, and a picture of Jesus nailed to the cross, his bleeding heart painted on his chest, was pasted to the back wall.

I studied his sad tear-stained face. I knew and believed that He had come down to this planet, died, and rose to life again, returning to heaven, but did He want more from me then to just believe all of that?

That evening while camping in a field of daisies I pondered the most famous verse in the Bible—John 3:16—". . . that whoever believes in Him . . ."

But I did believe in Him! Why didn't I have peace then?

My mind was flooded with questions, but I was too tired to think anymore. Ilana had written to me, and she would be finished with her job at the ski resort in a few days. If I could meet her in Switzerland, we could travel together for the summer. So I headed to Switzerland to pick her up.

From Switzerland we spent a week touring along the French Riviera and into the small country of Monaco. Then Ilana and I decided to head north to Great Britain. In London we lounged in James Park, attending the outdoor band concerts while embroidering our jean pant legs, walking in Hyde Park, listening to the self-appointed speakers on their soapboxes, and sitting in the sun on the British Museum steps. In Wales a little old couple living on the street where we camped invited us to eat with them.

As we traveled, we talked nonstop. Ilana told me all about her trip to Israel, about her winter skiing, and about this guy she was writing to. Her family and his were old acquaintances from years ago in Israel. She had met him again on her trip there, and he was coming to Canada to see her. I told her about my journey out to Afghanistan, about Alain, and about our plans to meet again on the West Coast.

Traveling north to Scotland, we reveled in the vivid green rolling hills dotted with white sheep, the stone cottages with their tiny yards, and the broken remains of old castles. In Edinburgh I received a letter from Alain. He had been in London for a week and wanted to rejoin us for the rest of the summer! He would move on to central Europe and try to track us down there if he missed us in Great Britain. The date he was leaving London was the next day!

Just one day! We would beat the mailman to London, so Ilana and I drove straight through, arriving at the American Express office the next afternoon. Of all things, there was Alain walking out, having checked the mail the last time for word from us! We were so happy to be together once again. The three of us merrily toured the south coast of England and then crossed back over the channel.

We dallied through Belgium, delighting in the flowers, the quaint village squares, and the canals in Bruges, our favorite Belgium village. In Amsterdam we found a quiet street where we parked next to a canal. It was only two blocks from Anne Frank's house. Every fifteen minutes the chimes rang out on the nearby cathedral, which helped lead us back to our camping street. We visited all the art museums, ate French fries on street corners, and sat in the town squares watching people.

On warm days we packed up and drove out into the country, sometimes washing our hair in a canal or rambling through little hamlets. The days flew by. Summer was nearly over. It was here that our trip truly came to an end.

A few months back on the beach in Aqaba, Jordan, we had met some French traveling kids. We received word from them asking if we could deliver the van to them in France. They wanted to buy it and would pay five hundred dollars for it. Yes, I wrote back. We could deliver the van to them in France. We would have to cross back over to Great Britain to catch our flights back to North America anyway, so we decided to meet them in Calais, France, at the ferry docks.

Ilana had to fly home to her job right away, so we saw her off once again, this time at the airport in Amsterdam. Our good-byes were jolly since we would see her soon back in the Northwest. But in France, it was very difficult to say good-bye to the old van, our home for the past year. The French kids were heading off on another trip, but we caught the boat to England where we spent our last night in Europe camped under some shrubs in James Park in downtown London. We were glad that it was August with little chance of rain.

Part Two

Into the Wilderness

"Where can I go to get away from you and the Holy Spirit?
Where can I run that you're not already there?
If I were to launch out into space, you'd be there.
If I were to tunnel into the depths of the earth, you'd be there.
If I had wings and could fly to the ends of the earth
or to the most remove island in the sea,
your presence would even be there
and your arms would be ready to hold me.
Even if I hid in the dark,
everything around me would be
as visible as day to you.
Darkness can't hide me from you because
the night is as light as the day to you."
Psalms 139:7-12

Alain and I had decided to stake our claim on Crown land in Canada. This idea first entered our heads while we were driving across the high plateau of Afghanistan. Since Alain had joined me on the West Coast in October, we were finding it difficult to re-adjust to civilized life after seeing how simply so many people lived in other parts of the world. Crown land was public land available for settlement. All we had to do was locate and stake the corners of the piece of land we were claiming, fill out the application, and send it in along with the marked map to the government offices. If approved, we would be given a certain amount of time to build a dwelling and occupy it. The maps we bought showed large sections available in central British Columbia. What appealed to us was that by living off the land we would be completely self-reliant.

Just a year ago, we had been living in a van in Europe. Now we were back on my farm in the Pacific Northwest making plans for a new quest together. This was all we thought and talked about.

Two facts helped us decide to move to Canada. First, Alain didn't have proper work papers to stay in the states any longer. In fact, the last time we had visited Ilana and friends north of the border, he hadn't been permitted legal re-entrance to the States. Since I had to get back to my job, I had to leave him in Canada. Later a friend drove him to the border and dropped him off in the woods between the official entry ports. He had to bushwhack his way through underbrush, forest, and over fences during the middle of the night to get back across. We were leaving soon to move to Canada, and he was in the middle of helping me pack up the farm.

The other fact was that I was already a landed immigrant in Canada.

We spent the winter studying maps, looking for special tools, and buying equipment for survival in the wilderness. Hand saws, adzes, drills—all were sharpened and packed ready for the big move. We found a blue-enameled Monarch wood-cooking stove, a waffle maker to use on the top of a woodstove, and other gadgets to take the place of kitchen appliances. My prize possession was a stone wheat grinder. We combed bookstores looking for books on building cabins, fences, and root cellars. We were more than ready to set out.

In the spring before we sold my little farm, we had made a trip to scope out the area we had marked on the map of central British Columbia. We had already traded in the car for a huge industrial-strength four-wheel-drive pickup with a front-loaded cable winch strong enough to pull up tree stumps. We threw some camping gear into the back and headed north.

Our first choice for homesteading turned out to be a big disappointment—the piece of land was mostly a huge swamp. My aunt and uncle were managers of a cattle ranch on Tsuniah Lake further west, so we headed there, knowing that they were snowed in but figuring we could hike in to see them and check out that area at the same time. We parked where the open road ended and camped in the back of the pickup overnight. In the morning we packed a couple of cheese sandwiches and, with the dog, began the hike in.

Within an hour we came to a fork in the road. The faint snowmobile tracks we had been following since we left the truck took the left fork. We were reluctant to turn that direction since the map, though vague, showed the ranch no more than five miles straight ahead, but we turned anyway, figuring that a used trail was more meaningful than a non-used one.

Up and down small hills we hiked, and by early afternoon we were sinking into the softened snow every few steps. But then we heard some muffled chopping through the trees, and we hurried our pace. The view opened up, and we could see a figure across a snowy meadow. We hollered but got no response, so Alain decided to hike closer. The snow was so deep and soft cross-country, it was easier for him to lie down and roll down the slope. The figure noticed the commotion and moved toward us. It was an Indian wearing a big black cowboy hat with the bowl punched round, shiny smooth black hair braided down his back, carrying a rifle in one hand, and wearing a red and black plaid wool shirt.

He hiked toward us and then right on past us with nary a word! We fell in behind him, and I filled the silence with what I did best, talking.

"Thank goodness we found someone! We are trying to get to the cattle ranch. Is this the right direction?" He just kept hiking.

"Do you know Flaten? He is my uncle. They don't know that we are coming to see them," I jabbered on. Not a word of response.

I tried speaking slower. "Is this the way to the ranch? On the map it looks like it is only three or four miles. We didn't realize it would be so far." Silence.

Suddenly the trail opened up onto a large meadow with a small log cabin situated halfway across, a horse corralled beside it. Without a word, the Indian strode toward it, opened the door, walked in, and straddled the only chair next to a table sitting under the only window. We stood hesitantly in the doorway, not sure of the protocol. Then we sidled on in and sat on the two boxes against the wall. And because nothing better came to mind, I resumed my jabbering, pouring out a summary of our past, present, and future, hoping to hit upon a magic word that would open some sort of communication.

Ignoring Alain's nudges to keep quiet, I again asked, "So is this the way to the ranch?"

It was then that the Indian slowly raised his arm and pointed out the window to the west. The land dropped down slightly, and we could see far in the distance over the forest of treetops, some faint lavender mountains. I was so pleased to get a response. I got back to business.

"So Flaten lives over there, right?" I pointed toward the mountains. He pointed toward the mountains too.

"How far would you say it is?" He pointed toward the mountains.

"Five miles?" I eagerly asked, but by now I didn't expect an answer. He pointed to the mountains.

"One hour?" This I asked hopefully because it was already mid-afternoon, and it got dark early in the spring that far north. By now he was just keeping his arm propped up, pointing toward the mountains.

"Shouldn't there be a big open spot for a twelve mile long lake? It looks like that doesn't happen until the bottom of those mountains, and they must be at least twenty miles from here. Do you think we can get there before dark?" He dropped his arm.

As we headed into the dim forest, following a very faint skidoo track, we could see his outline in the window watching us as we traveled toward the mountains. The trail followed a continual gradual descent. We hiked on and on and on. We had eaten our cheese sandwiches hours before we met the silent Indian. At least the snow wasn't bogging us down like it did on the open trail, for the thicker trees had kept the snow from piling up. We couldn't see the mountains to judge our progress because of the evergreens, but they had faded with the dusk anyway.

By then Alain wasn't talking much, just putting one foot in front of the other. At one point he slumped down onto a stump and announced he couldn't go any further. Even the dog was tired. On and on we hiked, miles and miles of my pep talks. "Look, it could be the lake up there! I see something! Hey, here is a fence! We have to be close now!

I am sure we are almost there!"

We were seeing increasing signs of cattle, tracks, fences, gates, and stacks of hay. The lake was a long one, so we shouldn't miss it. We were now sloshing through slush, and our boots were full of water, but we didn't really care any longer. It was dark, but the whiteness of the snow helped the light linger a little longer. We had gone through seven or eight gates with no sign of life, but suddenly there in front of us was a log cabin. Smoke was pouring out of the chimney, and a voice could be heard saying, "Well, look what the cat drug in! Where in the world did you come from?"

It was my uncle! He couldn't believe his eyes! We couldn't believe our eyes! My Aunt Dorothy couldn't believe her eyes! We had been hiking more than ten hours and had covered over fourteen miles. The Indian we had met was Casmir. He spoke little to no English. Three days later, well rested and fed, my uncle took us out by horseback on the proper trail back to our truck. We didn't find our land, but we did chew on a big piece of wilderness.

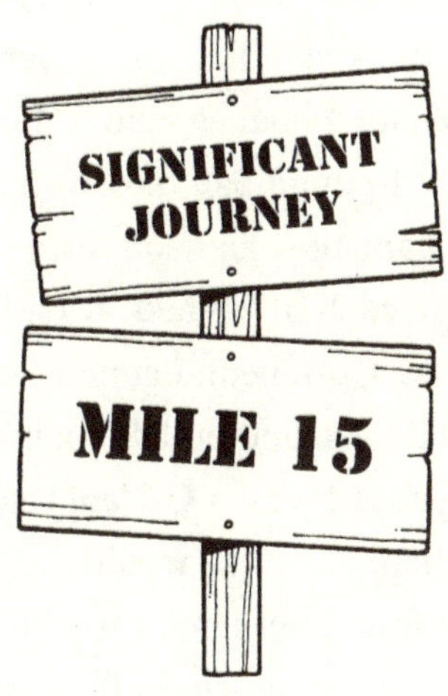

It was June, and we were packing up my small farm. I had sold it, and we were on our way north. Since our spring trip, we were even more determined to find a piece of land, stake it, and live self-sufficient. We felt we were well-read about homesteading, how to store food, what tools we would use, and how to live without power and running water.

The horse trailer held my horse, Jet, who we would use for transportation in the wilderness. My Afghan Hound, Jappeur, rode regally on the front seat. The back of the pickup was filled with cages holding twenty-three chickens and a rooster. Another cage held our cat, Molly. The mother milk goat, Madame, and her three kids occupied the space in the middle. The last cage held two rabbits who we were raising for fur to make clothing, socks, or blankets. They were a special breed called Red Satin, for we figured there was no reason to wear ordinary rabbit fur.

The goat was for milk. The cat was for keeping us free of rats, and of course, the chickens were for eggs. The dog would be for safety. We hadn't figured out what the baby goats would be for. Otherwise, we felt we had thought of everything for living off the land in Canada.

During the past winter, we kept track of the amounts of food we used. So we were well-stocked with apples, four forty-pound boxes of Kings, Gravenstein, Winter Bananas, and Yellow Delicious. We had also purchased a hundred-pound bag of carrots, the same of potatoes and onions, and some cabbages and squashes. A hundred pounds of wheat berries and a case each of canned string beans, peas, corn, and tomatoes were stuffed in. Cornmeal, oatmeal, sugar, oil, raisins, salt, some herbs, spices, fishhooks, and bullets rounded out our supplies.

Alain would go on ahead with a U-Haul truck carrying our stove, household furnishings, and tools. He would drop them off at a storage place up north until we found our land. I was to drive the pickup with the horse trailer. On our scouting trip in the spring, we found a good place where I could park and camp with the animals in some trees under the Trans-Canada highway. That was where I would wait for him when he brought the rental truck back to the states since it could not be taken one way into another country.

I arrived at the border crossing with no trouble. It was a few minutes after four on a hot late June afternoon. The veterinarian who checked animals entering Canada had just gone off duty and wouldn't be back until eight in the morning. I hadn't counted on that complication. I would have to wait for him to check my animal papers.

"Hmmm, I have this load of animals. Would it be possible to park over there to the side until morning?" I cautiously asked the border person. It was the first time I had driven a trailer, and I had no idea how to back it up and turn it around.

"Well, OK, just don't let any of the animals out."

Luckily I had a book to read. Unluckily, I had forgotten my sleeping bag and pillow. They were on their way north in the rental truck. I had also forgotten my toothbrush, comb, and extra clothing, essentially everything I took on a trip. But at least I had a book to read. It was hard to concentrate on it with the horse shifting his weight and rocking the truck, the goats "baaing" to get out, and the cackling of the chickens. At least the rabbits were quiet, and so was the cat, who, I noted, was curled into a tight psychotic ball in her cage.

Watching the big commercial trucks passing by, I wondered if I could pass for a professional livestock mover or some such thing. But then I remembered the mattress sticking out of the horse trailer. Resigned, I slumped down in my seat, attempting to immerse myself in my book. Slowly the afternoon dragged into evening.

I didn't sleep too well. The dog took up too much space, and the truck seat wasn't long enough to stretch out. The sucking noises of airbrakes from the continual line of commercial trucks slowly moving through customs and the rooster crowing every little while kept me awake. So at dawn I got up, ran my fingers through my hair, and contemplated how I would manage milking the goat, the main obstacle being how I would crawl over the tailgate without letting the three kid goats out.

One thing I hadn't counted on was the eggs. We had twenty-three good laying hens. I was startled to see eggs lying here and there and everywhere in the truck bed, having passed easily through the cage bottoms. Most of them could be described as "shell challenged."

But at the moment I needed to milk the goat. Vaulting into the truck and slapping shut the hatch, I landed on my hands and knees in a slime soup of animal product that would soon reach a simmer as the day warmed. It took my breath away. I wouldn't be able to milk the goat in there. I was not thinking clearly after the bits and pieces of sleep I had, but I did know that I couldn't let one goat out without the rest following because that was what goats do.

So what was I to do? I tied them together in tandem on one rope, slithered to the ground, goats in hand, slinked around to the far side of the truck, tied the other end of the rope around my ankle and milked the goat. The real trouble started when I tried to get them back into the truck.

At least the two rabbits were behaving. Flattened out on their stomachs in their cage side by side, their silky red fur shone in the early morning sunlight. The cat gave me a disgusted look. I had to put her in a cage for this trip, and she was definitely not a happy camper. I had the feeling she couldn't handle too much more of this ark-like adventure.

I glared at the rooster. His needless crowing woke me way too early, and I didn't appreciate it. The chickens were raising such a ruckus that it was hard for me to keep a low profile. The truck driver in front of me in the line-up kept eyeing me out of his rearview mirror.

It was 7:40 a.m. when I had moved into the customs line-up. I reeked, but I had the sheaf of precious animal immigration papers with official signatures from the American veterinarians firmly in hand. We didn't realize that it would take four months to immigrate a chicken. Chickens hardly live longer than that. We were probably the only people under the sun who paid a quarter per chick, and then another two dollars each to immigrate them to another country. Trouble was, they all had names, and we couldn't leave friends behind.

The veterinarian was due to show up any minute. I glanced at my reflection in the rearview mirror, wiped some egg off my face, and rubbed some manure off my overalls. Everything was under control. But it was going to be another scorching day. I didn't want to open up the back of the pickup when the vet was there and discover that I had a load of heat-stroked animals, so cautiously I flipped up the canopy hatch, snapping a few goat noses to push them back.

Madame, the mother goat, was still miffed about my manhandling her earlier. In a flash, she snaked her head over the tailgate, yanked the sheaf of papers out of my hand, and in one smooth motion galloped to the other end of the truck. There she stood in defiance, braced for battle, glaring at me, sucking paper, staples and all, down her scrawny neck!

The vet showed up just as I was flattening out the mass of slobbery papers on the bumper. I had fresh manure on my elbows and egg shells sticking to the bottom of my shoes, but the signatures were still readable.

By 8:10 a.m. I was parked below the Trans-Canada highway in a nice shady grove of trees, a small clear creek running past, and hidden from view, never mind the dull roar of traffic overhead.

The first thing I did was tether the goats. They eagerly began to clear the underbrush. Then I unloaded the six chicken cages and gave them some grain and fresh water. The rabbits enjoyed nibbling grass blades coming through the bottom of their cage. I put the cat on the front seat of the truck and gave her some food and water. I tied the dog out under one of the trees, and he settled down for a nice nap.

The horse was the biggest problem. I got him out and walked him around to exercise him, but he had never been trained to be tied to a stake. He kept tangling himself in the rope. So, after I freshened myself in the creek, I set up my lawn chair, and, with my book in one hand, I held the horse's lead-rope in the other—I read and he grazed. Even with this arrangement, every few minutes I had to stop and untangle him.

There wasn't much to do once I got the animals comfortable. I had to stay there at least until the next day some time. I didn't have much hay for the horse since there wasn't room to carry it in the trailer, but I noticed a farm about a quarter of a mile away. I decided to lead my horse there and see if I could buy some hay.

Ignoring the farmer's amazed, puzzled, and somewhat cautious look, I made my request known. He kindly offered me as much as I could carry and refused pay. With horse in hand, I headed back to camp. The farmer was still standing staring after me as we turned into our grove of trees.

I was back in my chair reading, dangling the horse on his rope when suddenly three children burst out of the underbrush into my clearing. They were as startled as I was but were soon petting the goats. I tied the horse up short on the back of the trailer and got a rabbit out for them to pet. I could tell they were under the impression that I was some sort of traveling circus, judging from the types of questions they were asking. After they left we all got back to what we were doing. About an hour later I heard voices, and the same children burst back into the clearing, but this time there was a woman with them.

"My kids said that there were all these animals here, but I didn't believe them!" She looked embarrassed and apologized profusely. If only I had had a monkey, I could have charged admission.

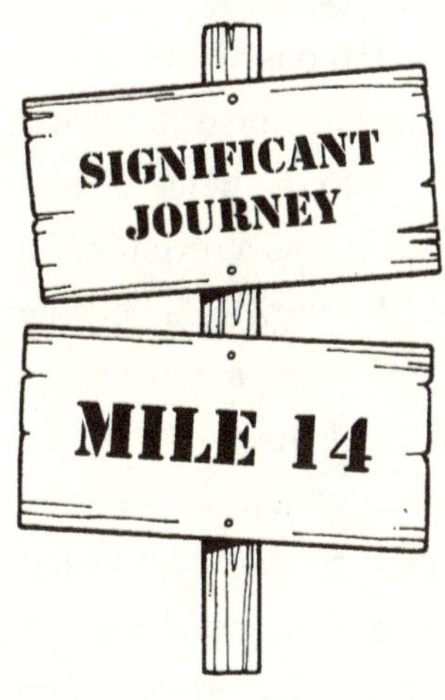

Alain arrived late the next day after returning the U-Haul truck and hitchhiking to where I was camping. We were back on the road together, heading up the Frazier River canyon. There were few places to stop, so by late afternoon we pulled into the first farm we came to and asked permission to camp in their yard. We also asked them if we could unload the horse and goats into their paddock. They graciously gave us permission, and the next morning after we loaded up, we paid them with lots of eggs before heading on our way.

We had been so focused on the move to the wilderness that we hadn't thought much further than that. It now began to dawn on us that we were going to need fences, shelters, and food for our animals when and wherever we decided to live. That meant we would need a temporary place to stay that had these things until we had done some building on our staked land. But even more serious was the fact that once we staked the land, we would have to wait for the approval from the government. So we made the decision to pull off at Gang Ranch. If we worked there, we would have a place to stay. We had heard of this ranch, one of the biggest in North America. Fortunately, there were jobs available, and we could leave our animals for a couple of days while we went to stake our land.

Leaving explicit instructions with the ranch hands who were in charge about never tying our horse on a long rope, we set up our animals and headed west into the wilderness. We had already located our five acres on the map. It was a nice piece high on a mountainside facing west with a beautiful view of a very large lake called Chilko. A creek ran along the north edge, and we would have access from the dirt road a few hundred feet below.

The following morning at sunrise we had staked all four corners, had marked it well on our map, and were headed back to Gang Ranch. Arriving by early afternoon, we found the horse tied in a stall, lying on the floor. The rope was wound around him so tightly that his neck was cranked around, his breath was labored and irregular, his neck was swollen on one side, and his legs were double their normal size. Our instructions had been ignored.

After cutting the ropes and untangling the horse, we forced him up and literally propped him against the wall. That was all he could manage for the first hour. His head kept swinging back to the position we had found him in, which kept causing him to lose his balance. We had to forcefully push and hold his neck in the normal position. The swelling gradually began to go down, and his breathing returned to normal. After another hour he was able to take a few steps. At the end of four hours, his equilibrium was back to normal, and he was able to negotiate some trips around the paddock. It was a close call.

Based on this episode, we, for once, made a smart decision. We decided to pack up and head to the cattle ranch on Tsuniah Lake where my uncle and aunt lived. Once there, we would rent one of the cabins until we got established. It was much closer to our staked land anyway.

It was only forty more miles to the ranch. We had just pulled off the main road and were headed to Tsuniah Lake where we hoped to stay for awhile. Still in sight of the Tatla Lake Ranch junction that maintained the post office for the area, a loud grating noise suddenly came from under the horse trailer, so Alain pulled over to the side. The shocks were broken. I walked the horse back to the ranch post office and got permission to put him in their pasture. Alain pulled the trailer slowly to the shop next to the post office. There, several men assured us that they could fix the problem, and by the next day we were on our way. By afternoon we had arrived at the Tsuniah Lake ranch. Exactly eleven days earlier we had left the little farm down south, about the same length of time it would have taken us in a covered wagon!

The setting was beautiful. The lake was a deep blue-green set in a valley between two rock mountain ridges. Not far to the west, we could see the snow-covered coastal range. Tall spruce grew in clumps forming fingers of black spires sloping down the mountainsides. Red-branched willows and heather made a thick mat along the shore. Stubby Douglas firs with stout trunks grew sparsely in rolling meadows of grass, allowing the moose, deer, and cattle plenty of grazing ground.

Tall thin Lodgepole Pines and white-barked Trembling Aspens made up the rest of the forest, but the broad grass-filled meadows gave the countryside a wide and expansive feel.

On the ranch were two livable cabins. The main one where my aunt and uncle lived was two stories high and backed by a couple of small shop cabins built of logs and rough-cut lumber. A tractor, dump truck, and odd pieces of farm equipment sat nearby. Several oil drums filled in spaces between.

The other livable cabin where we would live was situated about an eighth of a mile away. It was set on slightly higher ground, while the bigger cabin was closer to the lake. They both faced southwest toward the lake and mountains.

Combinations of Russell, Buck, and zigzag fencing surrounded the ranch buildings and enclosed several corrals fitted out with cattle-loading shoots. Except around the smaller paddocks, all the fences were built without buried posts because the ground was hard and rocky. When miles of fencing are needed over rough wilderness terrain this works the best.

A group of three smaller cabins down on the lakeshore was called the "Fish Camp." A dusty quarter-mile lane connected them with the rest of the ranch. The ranch owner, who lived in Oregon and was also a pilot, flew his friends and relatives up for a few days each summer and that was where they stayed. The grass-covered airstrip was built at the base of the mountains and ended almost at the edge of the lakeshore.

Our cabin was twenty feet square and divided into two rooms by a waist-high partition of logs. The floors were made of plywood, and the walls were chinked with fiberglass insulation that had to be routinely re-caulked. The only door opened onto a covered porch running the full-length across the front. The wooden kitchen counter held a sink with a faucet, but it was not hooked up to a water or drainage system. Fortunately, there was a chimney all ready for our cookstove, which we would use for heat and cooking. The outhouse was twenty feet away in a cluster of aspens. A clothesline ran from the house to one of those trees.

We carried our water from the creek. There were two creek branches, one going to the left of our cabin and the other going to the right. The right branch flowed to the main ranch house. Alain dug out a deep hole in ours to use as a refrigerator. We kept our goat's milk there in glass jars out of direct sunlight because the sun changed the taste.

There was a second smaller log cabin near our creek and a third tiny one directly across the creek from it. The little one was very old and dilapidated with no door. The birds flew in and out of its glassless window. We used the second cabin to store our animal feed because it had a locking door. We set up the rabbit cages next to it and built a lean-to shelter on the backside for the horse and goats.

Alain built a pen for the chickens. Because it was built into a dirt bank, it would stay warmer for them during the winter. Hawks and eagles swirled around overhead, hungry for easy pickings, so we fortified the top with a double thickness of chicken wire. He also dug a root cellar deep into the bank next to the chicken pen. It took Alain more than a week, shoring it up inside with hand-cut logs and roofing it with thick sod. In the summer it would stay nice and cool, and in the winter it would keep our food from freezing.

The first night we stayed in our cabin, it took awhile to get to sleep because of all the racket in the attic. We thought it might be mice, but neither of us had ever heard such noise from mice. In the middle of the night, I woke up with a start. Alain was standing in the middle of his army cot with the flashlight in one hand and his shotgun in the other.

"Something fell on my feet! I kicked it off, and it hit the ceiling . . . it was huge!" He said in a hush. "There it is! Here, hold the light!"

Two round eyes reflected white in the flashlight beam. They were definitely bigger than a mouse! His gunshot reverberated and echoed throughout the cabin and against the mountains outside. We didn't take the time to check out his shot. In less than ten seconds, we grabbed our sleeping bags, crammed on our boots, and rushed out the door. Splashing through the creek, we were pounding on the door of the main cabin in record time.

"Packrats!" Uncle Flaten announced sleepily. "The cabin's most likely full of them! Except for their rat-like tails, they look like squirrels and act like squirrels. In the morning we will set some traps and re-chink your logs good and tight."

"Here, spread out your sleeping bags in the living room on these mats." Aunt Dorothy fluffed up a couple of pillows as she handed the mats to us.

Rat-like tails. In spite of this image scampering around in my head, I fell asleep almost immediately. We would tackle trapping our unwanted guests in the morning.

I was glad my aunt and uncle were there to show us the ropes, but that arrangement wasn't going to last too long. Another manager was taking over the ranch that summer because my uncle and aunt were moving back south. Fortunately, Jack, the new manager, was happy Alain was there, and we got along just fine. There would be a crew of four or five Indians from Nemiah Valley and the surrounding area who would be helping with the haying, but Jack needed another farmhand. Some cattle were sold and shipped in the fall but a sizeable herd would be kept through the winter, along with a dozen horses. The hay was for them.

The haying began the next week. The wild meadows were located over a ten-square mile area. The terrain was rough, rutted, and lumpy. The hay was cut with a tractor, but raked and winnowed with a horse team.

One morning early Alain went out to get Blue, the part Belgium draft horse. She was a beautiful blue roan. He was to harness her to the hay rake, but he found her standing under a tree with a newborn black colt beside her. No one had known she was pregnant, and they didn't expect it because there were no stallions on the ranch. But legend had it that there was a wild one running with a herd of feral horses.

Jack was not happy. The owners did not want another horse, especially one with wild blood in his veins. We talked Jack into giving the colt to us. We named him Indigo.

It was quiet a few days later when I went out to milk the goat. Alain had left soon after daybreak with Jack to drive into Williams Lake, which was 180 miles away. They were picking up some machinery parts for the hay rake.

At that point my aunt and uncle were gone. But Aunt Dorothy had left me some books, a sourdough starter, and her recipe for delicious pancakes. We would miss them and their good advice about living in the wilderness.

Meanwhile, I was the only one at the ranch. The creek gurgled, the breeze rustled the leaves in the trees, and far away I heard a cow low. The aspens already showed a hint of gold. The breeze was cool and sharp on my cheek. It took only a couple of minutes to strain the milk, put it in a clean jar, and prop it up between some rocks in the shady creek to cool. An eagle cast his flying shadow across my path. I gazed up into the wide open sky.

Earlier I had ground wheat berries into flour in the stone grinder. It took an hour to grind about ten pounds of flour. After the first run through the grinder, I had to sift out the larger pieces and run them back through two more times. Then the flour was fine enough to make bread. The bread I had mixed and kneaded earlier had doubled in size in their pans, so I put the four loaves into the oven. I swept the porch and relaxed, reading in the hammock on the porch until the bread was done.

But nothing, not even reading, stopped my thoughts that day. As busy as I was with the chores, the wilderness was so wide and huge, so quiet, that it demanded that I think about my life, something I had avoided doing for years. It puzzled me that I still had not found peace and contentment.

Growing up in a Christian home and going to Christian schools, I had learned all about the lives of Samuel and Saul, Peter and Matthew, Esther and Ruth. The dates of the fall of Babylon, Persia, Greece, and Rome were still in my head. The beasts of Daniel and Revelation were vivid in my memory. I still knew all the Christian words like salvation, redemption, and deliverance. Phrases like "the nature of man," "the grace of God," and "the state of the dead" were as familiar to me as my own face. I knew wonderful Christian people including my own parents. Something was still missing. Here I was, the years flying by, and I still did not know what faith was all about or what Jesus wanted for my life.

There was something that needed immediate attention every day out in the wilderness, and usually it involved our animals.

One morning two Indians on horseback tried to bring a herd of cattle past our cabin. I noticed them all milling around, so I went outside to check it out. There was Madame, our mother goat, head down, facing off the whole herd, defying them to try passing her. It was kind of amusing, but the Indians showed no such emotion. It wasn't until I led her out of sight that the herd passed on by.

The fact was that I was concerned about Jet, our horse. I was worried about all the bites he had from the black flies, which were very thick. He was covered with bleeding welts, and I could tell that he had lost weight. The ranch manager said that the flies would thin out as summer waned.

Jet was trained for the show ring. For a couple of years, he and I had ridden the show circuit all over the Pacific Northwest. He was well trained. Jet was named after the Tennessee Walking Horse champion the year he was born. His name fit. He thought he was racing when he got into the show ring, but speed is not a feature judged in the Tennessee Walking Horse show classes. Since riding and showing horses was all new to me, it took all I had to hang on and stay put in the saddle, and I had no real idea how to slow him down.

One day a woman came up to me after a show and remarked, "We see you all over the state with your horse, and you always have a smile on your face."

I replied, "I am not really smiling, I am grimacing!"

There were other horses we could use, but Jet was smooth and comfortable to ride on the trails. So one day Alain took him out to go hunting. Forgetting that Jet didn't know much about guns, Alain took aim and fired at a deer while sitting in the saddle. It took Alain two hours to get back to the cabin—Jet beat him by an hour and forty-five minutes.

Jet didn't like getting his feet wet, and he especially didn't like to wade across streams. So another time Alain found himself in the creek on his back after Jet suddenly balked at a creek crossing. And once again, Jet left Alain in the dust.

One morning Jack stopped by our cabin early to see if I would help them round up the cattle and bring them down closer to the ranch. They were short of hands and horses to help in the roundup. Jet high-stepped between the trees and pranced through the gates, looking slightly out of place, but we helped keep the cattle from straying.

The rest of our animals gained notoriety in our neighborhood, especially Jappeur, my Afghan Hound who looked the most unsuitable to life in the wilderness. Anytime the cowboys brought horse or cattle herds past the cabin, I had to call him in. His quick movements, long swishing coat, and high curled tail spooked the cattle. He was the one animal we had who got the Indians animated. They laughed out loud every time they saw him.

The two rabbit cages had to be repaired every couple of days because the kid goats—Edelweiss, Ewell Gibbons, and Little Big Man—found them irresistible for jumping on. It must have been the upsetting of their cages that kept the rabbits from reproducing. It wasn't until September that we had our first baby rabbit, and it was an only child. We figured we might have to settle for fur socks instead of coats. But we also knew that neither one of us would have ever had the heart to skin one of our rabbits anyway.

The chickens were the hit of the neighborhood. We had dark brown Rhode Island Reds, golden New Hampshires, and speckled black and white Plymouth Rock chickens. The horses would snort and stamp if they had to pass by the chicken pen, and the cattle would switch their tails and show the whites of their eyes.

We put some Rhode Island Red eggs under our one Banty hen named Chloa. They hatched and quickly outgrew her. When she called them to her, they lifted her off the ground when they dove under her wings.

One nice thing about our wilderness home was that we all worked together to share our food supply. The guest fishermen at the fish camp brought us trout every day, and we furnished them and Jack with eggs. When the egg supply got ahead of the demand, we stored the extras in the root cellar in buckets filled with a clear liquid called "glassine."

Of course, there were other animals we had to deal with that were not so friendly. Everyone was concerned about grizzly bears. We were supposed to carry a can of rocks to rattle when we went out into the woods. At first I was not sure if grizzlies were a real concern or not. But then Jack called us over to the ranch house to show us a yearling calf he had found mauled by a bear. From that point on, Alain always carried his gun. If and when I went out of sight of the cabin, which I didn't do often, I carried on loud conversations with myself. A can of rocks was much too heavy to carry around everywhere I went.

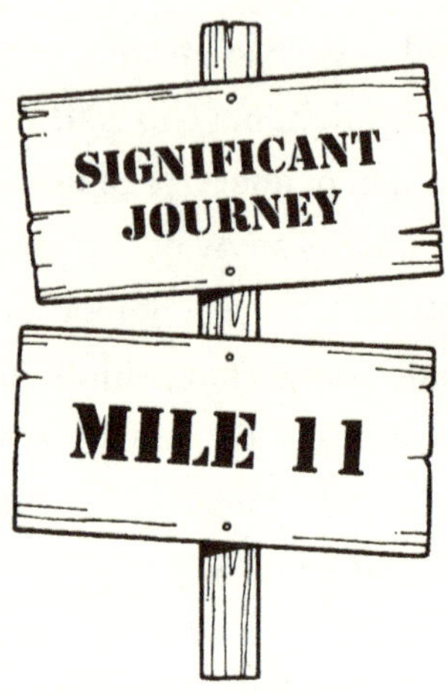

"Where do you find that story about Damascus and Paul in your Bible?" Alain asked one evening after dinner. We were sitting on the porch watching the goats play. The black flies were gone now that the summer days were shorter. The sun was low and the days were now cooling quickly.

This wasn't the first question Alain had asked me. A couple weeks earlier, he had taken the Bible out of a box of books and paged through it. A few minutes later, when I was feeding the chickens, he had come out and asked, "What is this teethe?"

I was puzzled until I took a closer look at the page he was reading. It was in the book of Malachi.

"Oh, tithe!" I then explained that it was one-tenth of our increase returned to God.

A few days later he was leafing through the Bible again and asked, "Who is this Satin?"

I knew it was Satan that he was inquiring about. He was reading in Revelation. He wanted to know where he could find more about him, so I showed him the Genesis account of Satan's deception of Eve and the introduction of sin on the earth.

That simple question about Damascus and Paul was why I began reading the New Testament out loud each evening after supper. For Alain, I also found the story of Paul when he was in Philippi. And that led to reading about Paul being arrested and put on trial in Rome. Alain eagerly listened, while I found the familiar words, filtered through his enthusiasm, taking on deeper meaning for me. It was late each night when we closed the Bible.

Alain had difficulty reading in English, so we sent word to my parents asking for a French Bible. But meanwhile he spent more and more time thumbing through the English Bible.

A picture began to form in my mind about this Man Jesus. My questions were slowly being answered. Not only was Jesus interested in all that I did, He knew everything about me, even before I was born! And it was there in that rough cabin in the middle of the vast wilderness that Alain and I both began to get acquainted with this Person named Jesus.

The hay was all stacked and covered. The crew had all gone home. Alain headed out to Tatla Lake to get mail and use the phone to call family. There was a pay phone in a booth there at the post office. At the small general store next door, he picked up some matches and some odds and ends. It took two hours to negotiate the forty miles of chuckholes and gates.

On his way back, he saw a nice mule deer standing by the side of the road, so he pulled over to watch him for a few minutes. The deer nonchalantly walked up to the open truck window and stuck his nose into Alain's hand. Slowly Alain opened the door and got out. The deer just stood there not more than three feet away, chewing his cud and watching him.

It was then that the thought entered Alain's head, "I will take this deer back to Judy. She would like it for a pet."

So, getting a rope out from under the seat, he carefully tied a big loop in one end, walked up to the deer, and dropped it over his head. Instantly the deer turned into a wild bucking bronco, throwing his feet up into the air and almost yanking the rope out of Alain's hands! He fought his way over to the closest pine tree and wrapped the rope around it. Next he used all his strength to reel the deer in close enough so that he could use his knife to cut the rope loose. The rope fragments scattered on the ground. The deer stopped struggling, shook himself, gave one outraged backward look at Alain, and dashed off into the forest, most likely never to gawk around humans again!

My days were half gone with just the daily chores. After feeding the chickens, goats, rabbits, cat, and dog, I would come back to the cabin and turn on the radio while I worked. The radio became an important part of my day. Daily the same people talked on the various programs, and I began to feel as if I knew them personally. But at noon especially it was very important to tune in to the Williams Lake station, which was 180 miles away, because they relayed messages to those of us out in the bush. To hear them say, "To Alain and Judy at Tsuniah Lake," was very exciting. Anyone passing through from the Tatla Lake post office brought us our mail, but this was less than once a month. The radio was the only way our friends and relatives could reach us on a daily basis.

Although we were so isolated, we were fortunate that our goat Madame was a good producer. She gave us about a gallon of milk per day. I decided to make cheese out of her milk. The recipe book on wilderness living contained directions, so I decided to give it a try. The process took up the whole morning. I had to heat the milk, strain it, wrap it in cheesecloth, and press the water out of it, but in the end I had this nice round ball of compacted cheese. I was supposed to let it age in a cool place, which was a bit of a problem. The only place I could think of was in one of the cabin cupboards. Alas, the temperature wasn't consistent enough, and I was left with a moldy ball of curds that bounced when I threw it in the garbage.

Every chore took longer out in the wilderness. Washing clothes took a full day. First, Alain and I would fill all our empty buckets at the creek and haul them to the cabin. I filled all my pots and pans with water and heated them on the stove. I was always glad that the weather was cooler on wash day because I didn't like to keep the stove going when it was hot out. I would then take the clothes out on the porch and squish them up and down in the biggest bucket. When it was winter, I had to also heat water to rinse them in, but in the summer I just put the washed clothes into the empty buckets and hauled them all down to the creek to rinse them.

Wringing them out was the worst part of the whole job. The creek water was so cold that my hands froze, and I had to take many breaks to warm them up. Then I would haul all the clothes back up to the clothesline and hang them up. They dried fast in the summer because it got pretty warm out and the humidity was low, but in the winter, they would freeze on the line before they had time to dry. Then I would bring them into the cabin and stand them around the stove, the shirts looking like short people warming themselves by the fire.

Not that anyone would have cared out there in the wilderness if we had run around in wrinkled clothes but ironed shirts felt better. I had a set of old-fashioned "sad irons" that I heated on the top of the woodstove. I had a couple of different kinds. My oldest model was a one-piece molded iron, but the whole thing, including the handle, heated up, and I had to use an oven mitt to hold it. My favorite iron had a metal frame with a handle that clipped onto the heavy solid bottom sections which had heated up on the stovetop. I had two of the bottom sections so that I could have one heating while I ironed with the other. It took a lot longer than with an electric iron because the iron cooled down pretty fast, but I still liked my clothes crisply pressed. I also used my treadle sewing machine to mend and patch our clothing.

Late in the fall, when the frozen road was easier and faster to drive, we decided to take a trip to see some of the other places in the Chilcotin area of British Columbia before we got snowed in. We could also check at the Tatla Lake post office for the French Bible we had asked my parents to find for Alain. It wasn't there yet, so we headed to Bella Coola, a settlement we were curious about that was located on the coast west of us. It would be nice to see the ocean.

Once out on the highway, we found that it was not paved going west. And when it got to the edge of our high plateau, it dropped severely to sea level. The road was so steep and narrow, and the switchback turns were so sharp that it took three turns, backing up each time in order to negotiate some of the corners. There were fourteen switchbacks. It was so scary that I got out and walked each one while Alain navigated the truck around alone.

The smell of the ocean was invigorating and the salt air felt soft on our faces as we arrived in Bella Coola. Fruit tree orchards and small farms were spattered around the long valley. The garbage dump was a big attraction. Many folks were out watching the black bears there. We joined them. Two days after we got back to the ranch we had our first big snow and the road out was no longer drivable.

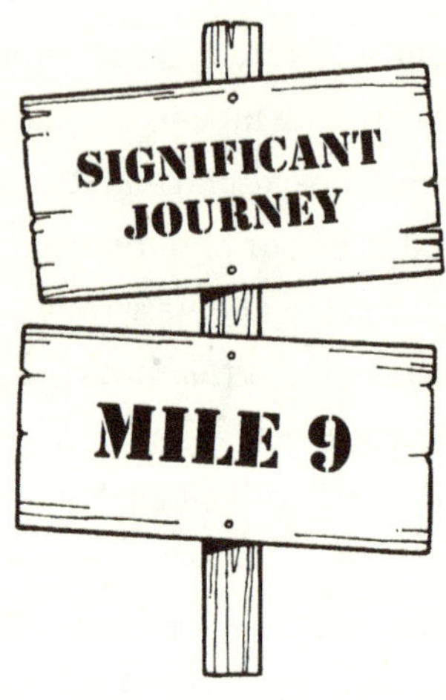

The owner of the fly-in fishing lodge and resort called Tsuniah Lake Lodge at the other end of the lake sent word down asking if Alain and I were interested in being the caretakers there for the winter. When the summer season began again next June, we could return to the ranch and help in the hay season. It sounded like a good idea. There wasn't much that had to be done at the ranch that Jack couldn't handle alone. Alain would get paid for each cord of wood he cut, split, and stacked at the resort during the winter, and we would have a furnished cabin with space to keep our animals. We would leave our things just as they were in our ranch cabin.

Alain made several trips along the lake to the resort, hauling our food, the things we would need for the winter, including my treadle sewing machine, and a ton of hay for the animals. On the last trip, he hauled our cat, chickens, goat, and rabbits in the truck, while I bundled up and rode the horse. The dog followed, trotting along behind me. Our three baby goats, then grown, had been sold a week earlier to a rancher in the next valley over, so we had only our mother goat, Madame. Indigo, the part Belgium colt, wasn't weaned yet, so we left him with his mother, Blue, at the ranch.

Because of the snow, ice, and mud, Alain had to winch the truck out of deep ruts in several places. Hooking up to trees and boulders, he inched along. The twelve miles took a little more than an hour one way each trip.

We moved into the largest cabin, which had three rooms with vaulted ceilings and was heated by a woodstove. We used an unheated fourth room for storage. The tree groves around the lodge protected us from the winds blowing up off the lake. We had a gas stove to cook on, and there was a big braided rug on the living room floor. The outhouse was close by the front door.

The main lodge building was built on the brow of the hill overlooking the lake. It sat right in front of our cabin. Inside the lodge the huge stone fireplace chimney covered one whole wall. A balcony overlooked the great room and wrapped around two sides. A tabletop game something like a miniature curling game was in one corner and bookcases lined another wall. The lodge housed six guest rooms, plus a dining room, kitchen, and large pantry. A big covered veranda ran outside across the front facing the lake and mountains. The row boats were lined upside down on the veranda, resembling tiny whales all in a row.

There were a half dozen other cabins sprinkled through the pine trees around the lodge, several smaller storage buildings, and a large new shop building. There was a water reservoir on the side of the mountain, which they used during the summer when it was not frozen, a corral, and a large grassy airstrip running out to the west. A short distance beyond the very end of the airstrip was Chilko Lake, which was fed by a creek running over from our lake, Tsuniah.

Against the back of one of the storage cabins, there was protection from the winds off the lake, so Alain used wire fencing we brought with us and some discarded lumber to build a chicken pen. The wire fencing covered the top of the small chicken yard to hinder predators. He set up a small woodstove inside the lean-to pen and ran the pipe out the side.

We would need the stove for when the temperature dropped later in the dead of winter. Once the chickens were set up, he began working on a dog house, peeling the small logs and caulking the spaces between with thin strips of pinewood.

The ton of baled hay we brought with us was used for walls inside the shop to make pens for the goat and the horse. We kept them fastened in each night and let them out during the day to run around. But the two of them mostly hung around the cabin, watching me through the cabin windows or resting under the trees where the snow had been swept away by the wind. The cat peered arrogantly at them from her perch on the dining room windowsill. As soon as we were settled, the lodge owners fired up their plane and flew out to their home in Williams Lake.

Life again settled into a routine of caring for animals, cutting firewood, hauling water, and fixing food. The evenings were long, but they were a welcome break after all the time we spent outdoors every day. Just before we left for the lodge, the French Bible was dropped off by a rancher passing through with a cattle herd.

So now Alain had time to open it. This was the first Bible he had read. In his home growing up, the Book was treated more like an icon or charm, but it was not opened. So I was interested in seeing what he would make of its contents and what conclusions he would draw from his reading.

I had been reading out loud from the English Bible for some time now, but I was interested in Alain's response as he read for himself. The more we read the more I found myself growing more and more interested in what Jesus said about everything, but especially what He said about peace. We were now in the book of John, and I had just read where He said, ". . . I want you to have the same inner peace that I have. . . that abiding peace with the Father that only I can give . . ." (John 14:27).

I was eager to learn more. Could I have that kind of peace as well?

There was another road running south from our lake to Nemiah Valley on Chilko Lake. From there, the road was kept open out to the main highway to Williams Lake all winter. This route was a lot shorter, only fourteen miles to Nemiah Valley versus the forty miles to Tatla Lake. There was no store or post office there, but if we left our truck parked in that valley, in case of emergency we could snowmobile out to it and then drive back to civilization.

As soon as the animals were set up, we locked the goat and horse in the corral to keep them safe, packed a lunch, took the dog, and drove out early one morning. We also loaded up our cross-country skis, figuring they would come in handy hiking back from the valley. We passed our staked land, but we didn't take the time to hike up to it since we needed to be back to the lodge by evening.

A lot of stories traded between folks out there reached mythical proportions after being repeated again and again. The story of Frank the hippie was one of those stories. Over hot tea, the rancher and his wife who agreed to let us park our truck at their place for the winter told us about this guy who had gone AWOL from the U.S. Army and moved into a teepee on the side of the mountain overlooking Chilko

Lake. In fact, we were told, it was the same mountain we had passed that morning on our way over, which was not that far from our staked land. We heard how he almost starved his first winter up there, but that the Indians had kept him alive by giving him meat from their hunting trips.

One time his mother had driven up in a big white Cadillac and tried to talk him into coming home. But he was happy with his life, growing his own marijuana and living off the land. Sometimes years went by without anyone seeing him.

We were on the road again by eight the next morning, plenty of time to hike the fourteen miles back to the lodge. The trees lining that section of road kept the snow from piling up, so not only had it been faster to drive but it was easier to hike. Of course, this created its own problem—there wasn't enough snow to use the skis, so we had to carry them slung over our shoulders.

"Look, there are foot tracks in the snow here!" I whispered. We were already a couple hours from the valley and it was startling to see human tracks suddenly appear out of nowhere. In fact, not only were they human tracks but they were barefoot human tracks, disconcerting to say the least out in the middle of the wilderness.

"It has to be Frank, the hippie," Alain whispered back. And sure enough, we rounded the corner and there was this bearded, barefoot guy, long hair askew, dressed in a faded plaid shirt and tattered jeans. He had his arms outstretched and was gazing toward the sun while standing in the middle of the trail!

"Hi," I said casually, and a bit cautiously.

He didn't respond coherently. Instead, he mumbled something about the clouds or the blue sky or birds; we couldn't exactly discern his words.

We were not sure of the protocol. What should we do? Try to strike up a conversation, invite him to hike along, walk on by, or what?

Naturally, I attempted to strike up a conversation. But none of the regular comments seemed appropriate, such as "Nice day for a walk isn't it?" or "Are you going our way?"

It didn't take us long to realize that Frank was living in his own little world and hadn't the foggiest notion that we were there beside him. Reluctantly, because I would have loved to know what was going on in his head, we bid him good-bye and hiked on, ruminating on the fact that we had seen a rare sight that not many folks had seen, a sight pretty much in the same category as the abominable snowman!

The road followed the lakeshore, sometimes climbing up high, opening upon breathtaking views of the coastal mountains, sometimes dipping down to a stream, but we didn't stop to sightsee because we needed to make use of every minute of daylight. This time, remembering our hike into the ranch last spring, we packed more food, which we ate as we kept moving. By mid-afternoon, our lunch packs were lighter, but the skis had gotten heavier. I was tempted every few feet to drop them by the roadside. I hoped we were almost home.

"This looks like the creek just before the airstrip," I announced, wading across.

"This MUST be the creek just before the airstrip," I hollered again as I jumped over another creek.

"No, maybe THIS is the creek just before the airstrip." I was sure this time.

"This HAS to be the creek just before the airstrip!" I declared for the dozenth time.

By then it was pitch dark. The only thing that guided us was our morning truck tracks on the roadway, which were faintly outlined by the now barely discerned whiteness of the surrounding scuff of snow. Dusk had dropped fast several miles back. It had been dark for nearly three hours. Fourteen miles seemed pretty short this morning. But it was a much different story now. Not only were we dragging our feet, but we were getting more anxious with each passing minute.

"Why don't I hurry on ahead to the lodge, get the jeep, and come pick you up," Alain said.

I agreed and Alain strode on ahead, energized by my assurance that I would be fine. His footsteps faded quickly. I was totally alone in the murky black of a wilderness night where all I heard were my feet hitting the frozen ground. But then, there was that strange sigh off to my left, an irregular rustle off to my right, and a peculiar burble behind me. Wondering which were bears and which were cougars, I tried to focus on my feet and tune my ears instead to the sound of a jeep engine, all the time hoping and expecting to reach that creek just before the airstrip.

It was then that I remembered. I was not alone. I believed in God. I didn't just believe IN God, I now believed God when He said, "I will not forsake you." He was watching out for me and cared for me. I knew that now.

Then I heard it, the faint drone of an engine, slowly growing louder. Then bursting between tree trunks, the headlights appeared, and in fifteen minutes we were back at the cabin, stoking the fire, heating up some soup, and laughing out of pure relief.

Things were slowing down. There was little water running in the creeks and what there was ran under a thick casing of ice. An occasional bald eagle soared in on the wind to sit above the outlet of the lake when we were down filling our buckets. We got our water out of the lake by the dock, which was just below the lodge knoll. The lake was lined with ice the day we moved in and then frozen solid across in a matter of days.

By November the lake ice was three feet thick. Because it froze so fast, it froze clear, giving us the uneasy feeling of walking on a fragile glass tabletop. Alain, growing up next to a big lake in Quebec, reassured me that I wouldn't fall through. But I never got used to the loud rifle cracks that whipped and snaked with lightening speed in the ice from shore to shore as the temperature dropped. Those cracks left frozen zigzag slices at various depths in the ice, which added to my concern.

We cut a hole in the ice to get our water. Because this hole froze over every night and had to be re-opened every morning, we kept an axe in a box on the dock. Of course, because of the snow, we couldn't really distinguish the dock from the lake except that it had a different sound when we walked on it. We not only had to carry water for cooking and cleaning but we had to carry water for all the animals. That meant many trips back and forth up and down the hill. We each carried two buckets to balance out our loads.

During the day Alain was either across the lake at the woodlot or out hunting. Sometimes I hiked along with him. We no longer had fish since the lake was frozen, so Alain hunted grouse since they stayed around all winter and were easy targets. They would sit in a row on a branch, so Alain would take aim and shoot one. As it would drop to the ground, the others would remain sitting but would look down as if to say, "Hey, we were talking to you! Where are you going?"

We also lived off of deer meat. Deer tracks were all around the cabin, so Alain didn't have to go far to bring one back. He hiked through a clump of pines one day while following tracks meandering through the stubby pine trees. A twig snapped, and when he glanced up, he was startled to find himself surrounded by a herd of twenty or more mule deer. He looked at them and they looked at him. Then as one, the deer all started striding deliberately toward him. They were big deer, and it wasn't a comfortable situation. But he had his gun and was able to startle them and bring home a deer.

We hung our meat in one of the other cabins where it stayed frozen all winter and was safe from coyotes and lynx. When we wanted to cook some, Alain would take an axe and chop off a piece. Jack, who was back at the ranch, traded us some venison for a hindquarter of moose. For some reason the moose spent the winter at his end of the lake. Our most common meal was stew with vegetables from the root cellar.

Every other Sunday Jack came down to our place by snowmobile for dinner, and the alternate Sundays we went up the lake to his place to eat. Traveling with snowmobiles on the smooth lake was so much faster than traveling during the summer on the deeply rutted roads. It didn't take long to cover the twelve miles. The snowdrifts on the lake would slow the machine down, but when it hit the clear ice, it would fishtail. And fishtailing at forty-five miles per hour down a frozen lake two hundred miles from a hospital was not my idea of a good time. In fact, Alain traveled so fast that Jack said that every Sunday he knew when to turn the tea water on because he could hear me screaming for Alain to slow down when we were still five miles out.

We traded books and discussed everything under the sun. Jack had invented several things—he even engineered and built a bridge over a wide river. He was good at solving problems. He did not believe in God, and we were surprised at this since he had lived so close to nature his whole life. Wouldn't it be hard to not believe in God seeing all of this beauty out here?

One weekend it was our turn to host Jack for dinner. The week before he had fixed us his delicious cornbread and moose stew. He was an excellent cook. He had been a bachelor out in the wilderness his whole life, but he enjoyed a good meal. I decided to roast a chicken as a treat after all the wild game we were used to. My cast iron Dutch oven pot held one chicken surrounded by a pot full of vegetables. We had no way to let Jack know when dinner would be ready, so when it was done, I turned the oven off but left the chicken in to keep it warm. Later when he arrived and we were ready to eat, I discovered that the chicken had shriveled to not much more than a small tough bite each.

One Sunday we went down early to Jack's place. About an hour before dark, we decided to head back to the lodge after spending the whole day there. The trail between the lodge and the ranch followed a low bank along the lake. Just as we were climbing on the snowmobile, out from that trail tottered Madame our goat!! She had walked the whole twelve miles through the wilderness in the snow! We couldn't believe our eyes! It was a wonder coyotes hadn't killed her. She was dead-tired, so Jack put her in his shop over night with some hay and water. The next day, he tied her in an open box on the back of a sled, propped her with hay bales, and hauled her back down the lake with his snowmobile.

November flew by, and soon it was Christmas Day. Alain brought in a chicken, plucked and cleaned, and I put it in the cast iron pot in the oven to cook with carrots, onions, and potatoes. I peeled some apples and made a pie in the afternoon. The day before, I had finished the sweater I had been knitting when Alain was out working on the firewood, and it was now under the tree with his name on it. I individually wrapped up the blue-striped socks, scarf, and cap I had made so that he would have more gifts to open. The comic sections of an old newspaper served as wrapping paper. My gifts looked cheerful tied shut with red yarn. I was surprised to notice a big box under the tree with my name on it! I had been puzzling all morning as to what it could be.

Our huge tree touched the vaulted ceiling. It took up most of the space in the living room and was all out of proportion to the tiny plastic nativity scene I had set on the trunk beside it, but no matter, it smelled like the holidays.

As soon as we had finished dinner, we exchanged gifts. I was not sure if Alain was real excited about the outfit I made him, but he put the things on and danced around the room pretending to be skiing.

"Where in the world did you get these?" I exclaimed when I opened the big box. I couldn't believe my eyes! A pair of ice skates!

"I got them on my last trip out to Williams Lake," Alain responded with a smile.

I was glad we opened our gifts in the afternoon and on such a nice sunny Christmas Day. We dug out Alain's skates and ran down to the lake to try them out. We were definitely "snowed in" now for the winter with the last snowstorm. The wind had blown all the week before, drifting the snow up against the buildings, but clearing a maze of ice paths over the lake, so it was perfect for skating. Alain whirled and twirled, his new scarf blowing—with the blue, green, and purple tassels—around his neck, as he jumped the drifts separating the trails of ice. There was no doubt that he was born a French Canadian judging by his fancy maneuvers across the twelve mile long skating rink. I slowly skittered and slid while the dog, fur flying, chased Alain.

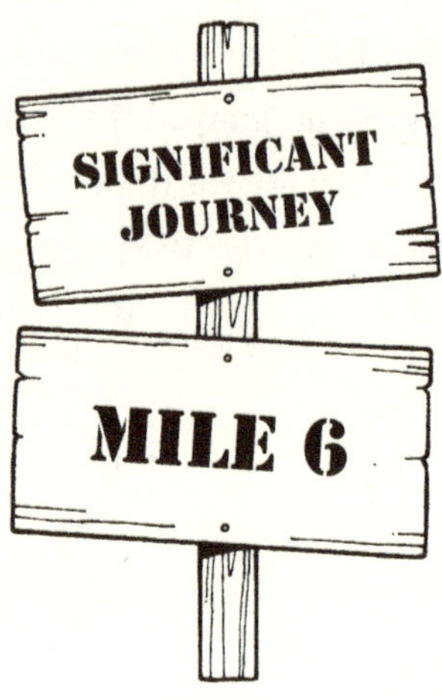

It was only minus fifteen degrees Fahrenheit with the sun shining. The air was very dry at our 5,000-foot elevation. It was the first day of the New Year. We sat at the kitchen table, warmed by the woodstove while drinking our lemongrass tea. The morning sun poured through the corner window. I started a stew in the cast iron kettle for lunch, and after Alain bundled up in his felt-lined boots and put the chainsaw on the back of the snowmobile, he headed across the lake to cut firewood.

At noon I tuned the radio to the Williams Lake station to hear the messages. Anyone could call or write to the station and send messages to anyone living out in the bush. That day I heard my name, a New Year's greeting from my folks!

When we finished lunch, Alain took the battery from the lodge jeep and hooked it up to the radiophone in the lodge office. The owner had shown him how to do it before he left in the fall. We were able to make connections first with my parents and then to Alain's. Our families were all fine. It was tricky speaking since there was a delay in transmission, and although we were shivering in the cold room where the radiophone was located, it was still hard to say "over and out" and hang up. We decided to call out once a month the rest of the winter.

The previous night the temperature had dropped below minus twenty, so Alain had started a fire in the chicken pen stove. He kept it going twenty-four hours a day. During the night he set the alarm and went out every two hours to stoke it with more wood. He would sit on a plank in the pen waiting for the fire to get going, and the chickens would crowd around him to keep warm. We expected it to get down to thirty below at night for the next month. The air was so dry that the fur on the animals crackled with static electricity.

We had to keep the cabin stove going around the clock also. The stove itself was made out of tin and often glowed red hot. But one morning the stove pipe also glowed and the red moved fast on up the chimney. We quickly closed off the damper on the stove, but it was too late. Smoke was pouring from the ceiling into the cabin. We ran outside and sure enough the roof around the stove pipe was smoldering. Alain rushed to the shop and got a ladder.

Meanwhile I brought out all the buckets and pans and filled them with snow. It would take too long to carry water from the lake. Once Alain got the roof area around the pipe packed with snow, the fire went out. It took us the rest of the afternoon to clean up the melted soot on the kitchen floor. It was a close call.

One day Alain decided to make sourdough bread. I had been using yeast for bread because the sourdough starter took a long time to make the bread loaves rise, although the starter was perfect for pancakes. So in the morning he mixed up the ingredients, kneaded the dough, and set two loaves in pans. He then let them rise, punched them down, let them rise again, punched them down, and let them rise a third time. They looked great. The only problem was it was near midnight when they were ready for the last rise, and he had to set the alarm to put them in the oven. Three o'clock in the morning, they were done, the bread turning out so beautiful that we took a picture of the loaves. But Alain didn't volunteer to make bread again.

February was just as cold as January. One fine day Alain called to me from the brow of the hill, “Judy, come look at the lake!”

My cake had just finished baking, so I pulled the pan out of the oven and turned it off. I then grabbed my parka and pushed my feet into my boots. What could be happening? Maybe he had seen a moose or something.

Breathlessly, I climbed up on the veranda of the lodge and shielded my eyes from the sun, all the while scanning the frozen lake for signs of something unusual. Alain was nowhere in sight, but then I saw him filling the water buckets at the water hole below me. It was then that my eyes focused on the lake surface. In the newly fallen snow in huge thirty foot letters, Alain had stamped out “I Love You!”

In a flash, Alain was up the hill. Gathering me in a big bear hug, he whispered into my ear, “So, will you marry me?” He had asked me in Crete, and he had asked me in Paris. This time I said yes!

Then I remembered that it was Valentine’s Day. I just had enough time to frost the cake before he brought up the water buckets.

One day in late winter Alain received a message over the radio station that his grandfather was not doing well. He decided to head back east to visit him. It had warmed up enough that our water hole in the ice was easy to open now, so I could get water from the lake without any trouble. He had cut a big pile of kindling, and I told him I would be fine alone. It was warm enough that I didn't have to keep a fire going in the chicken pen. I had the cat and dog for company. He would drive the snowmobile out the fourteen miles to Nemiah Valley where we had left our truck, and he would drive to the airport from there.

A few nights after Alain left, Molly, the cat, didn't come to the cabin to eat. I always kept her and the dog inside at night. I was not too concerned the first night, but when the second night came and she didn't show up, I began to worry. First, I looked for her around the barn and chicken pen, thinking she might have fallen asleep and gotten fastened inside by accident.

As the days went by, I unlocked and searched all of the buildings, thinking that perhaps Alain had gone into one of them and she had followed unseen. She was nowhere. She couldn't have drowned, I reasoned. The lake was still frozen. I couldn't think of anywhere else to look.

The days ticked by. It had been nine days since Molly had disappeared. Since it was just me there, I had no other person to ask if they had seen her. Well, there was God. He knew her and that was why I had been thinking of talking to Him about her, but it was strange to call on Him, especially since she was just a pet. And, I hadn't talked to God for a very long time. Actually it had been years. I thought it would be peculiar for a person like me, who hardly knew God, to ask for help about a pet cat. But she was a good mouser and a good friend.

But then I questioned, why involve God in the life of a cat? She was replaceable; cats are easy to come by. And maybe she was just fine. There were those nine lives she had to fall back on, right? Would God even hear my prayer? I had hardly given Him the time of day for the past eight years.

My mind mulled over these thoughts as I carried the water buckets down the hill to the lake. The temperature was dropping with the dusk. It was a frigid thirty degrees Fahrenheit. It always got so quiet as night came on. I hesitated, not wanting to hurry back to the empty cabin. Molly was gone. It was then that I bowed my head and self-consciously whispered into my hood.

"Dear Father, would You watch out for the cat? Thank you for listening. Amen."

It had now been twelve days since Molly had disappeared. I hurried out to fill the wheelbarrow with wood and roll it back to the door. The sun was out, and I glanced over to the windowsill where Molly liked to clean her paws on mornings like this.

It was then that I heard a small sound, a tweak of a sound, like a meow. I paused with an armload of wood, not daring to exhale. Moments passed. It didn't happen again. I sighed and turned toward the door.

There it was again. The sound of a cat's meow, and it seemed to be coming from the tree, up high, or from the roof . . . the roof of the lodge. There it was again—the meow of a cat!

"Molly, Molly! Where are you? Where in the world are you?"

She answered from somewhere on the roof of the lodge. I dropped my armload of wood, flew to the porch, raced up the fire steps, clamored over the snowdrifts draped from the eaves, and rushed toward the meow, much louder now. She was calling from the chimney! I grasped the stone rim and peered into the sooty depths. Luminous green eyes peered back. She was alive! Two minutes later I had reached her through the lidded but unused stove-pipe opening inside the lodge and rescued her.

"Thank you, God, for hearing my prayer!"

Years earlier, the summer after I had graduated from high school, few jobs were available for teenagers, and my parents had no funds to send me to college. Every day I prayed that it was God's plan that I should go. I was certain that my prayer would be answered.

The small amounts of money I earned babysitting were set aside for college. I wrote letters to people who might be interested in loaning me the college entrance fee. Then I spent my spare time sewing items to supplement my wardrobe.

But I received only "nay" answers to my inquiries for a loan. Three days remained before freshman registration closed, and the college was 300 miles away. That evening, seeing my packed trunk in the corner of my bedroom and noting my clothes all neatly pressed ready to load into the car, my mother sat down on the end of my bed and put her arm around me. She was concerned that I would be disappointed and hurt if I couldn't go to college. I reassured her that I would be going, that I was sure that God wanted me there, and that He would answer my prayers.

In the next day's mail was a letter with a check for five hundred dollars. It came from a man I had known as a child in Alaska. It was in answer to a letter I had written three months before but had long since given up on receiving an answer. He had been away from his home and just received his mail. He also promised to send another five hundred dollars if needed later in the school year.

My mom and I were in the car and on our way to college in less than an hour. I knew then without a doubt that God cared personally for me and answered prayer.

But it was not until God helped me find Molly in answer to my prayer that I remembered that answered prayer many years before.

One morning two Indians from Nemiah Valley stopped by our cabin. A week earlier Alain had returned from a month in Quebec. I knew he was across the lake cutting firewood, so it startled me to find someone at the door.

One was a girl. I had never had a female visitor stop by. They came straight in and sat down at the table. I set out tea, bread, and jam. While I was pouring hot water into a couple of mugs, they began to eat, silently. As always I started jabbering to fill in the quiet.

"So what are your names?" I paused expectantly as I took a seat.

"Where are you from?" I asked as I moved my chair in closer.

"Where are you going?" I continued on, hoping to hit the right question to get a response.

Finally, the guy answered and said, "She's my sister."

"Hi, my name is Judy, nice to meet you!" I turned to her with a smile, but I got no response.

"What is your name?" No answer.

"I'm thirty-one. How old are you?" Still I got no response.

Suddenly the brother spoke up and said, "She's thirty."

Just as quickly she replied, clearly and empathically, "No, I'm twenty-eight!"

I gave her a big smile. I understood. We women reach our thirties soon enough!

It was late on another day, one of the rare days when it was overcast. There was an abrupt knock on the door. And before I could get up from the rocking chair, it opened. It was the chief of the Indians from Nemiah Valley. He wore a big broad-rimmed black felt hat and a green plaid wool insulated jacket, and he carried a rifle. He had ridden in on horseback so quietly that I hadn't heard him arrive at all.

He was on his way from Tatla Lake forty miles northeast to Nemiah Valley, fourteen miles south, and he was bringing us our mail from the post office. Standing his rifle against the door jam, he sat down across from Alain at the table and drank tea and ate some big slices of bread with strawberry jam. Since he wasn't speaking much except for a nod or a grunt, I filled in the air space with chatter of this and that. Suddenly he got up and left, which was the way it always happened. Up at the ranch when this first happened to me, I thought that I had said something to offend the Indian visitor. But that was not it. The custom was that once they were finished with their tea, it was time to go. That was all.

This time though, just before he picked up his rifle and passed through the door, he turned and asked, "You seen my dog?"

Startled, I asked, "Did you lose your dog?"

He replied, "He not follow me when I go past here before."

"Ohhh, that is too bad. What does he look like?" I inquired.

"Looks like coyote."

Just then my eyes focused over his shoulder. Through the open door I could see the tree outside our cabin. On one of its branches hung the skin of a coyote, drying.

Yesterday Alain had rushed into the cabin out of breath, grabbed his rifle, pocketed some bullets, and said in a hushed voice, "I see the coyote who has been hanging around the chicken house. I am going after it!" Two minutes later I heard the shot and Alain came back dragging this dead coyote. He cleaned it outside. And then we spread a tarp on the floor so he could skin it where it was warm.

I kept remarking how much coyotes looked like dogs. It was a nice skin, thick and cream-colored. He skinned it out very professional-like, keeping the paws intact so that when it spread out on the floor it would make a nice rug. Then he hung the skin from the tree branch to dry.

"We will keep an eye out for your dog," Alain called as the chief mounted his horse and rode over the hill.

It must have been the cloudy sky combined with the descending darkness that kept the chief from seeing his dog hanging there in the tree. And it was under much deeper darkness that Alain took down the dog and gave it a proper burial. That half coyote rug wouldn't warm our hearth after all.

Rag rugs are so much easier to make anyway.

Back at the ranch with his mother, our part Belgium colt, Indigo, was finally weaned. It was time for him to move to our place, so the next Sunday when Jack came to dinner, he led the colt while he rode Calico, one of the ranch horses, followed by Lady, the cattle dog. We went out to meet him halfway. I rode Jet while Alain skied. Of course, Madame, the goat, followed in her manner, so close on his heels that he was jerked to a sudden stop every time she stepped on the backs of his skis. Jappeur, our dog, tagged along. Our "Pied Piper" group met Jack's group along the lakeshore where we had made previous plans to eat our Sunday picnic.

It was easy to find a wind-swept log to spread out our lunch with all the fixings. Hot potato soup warmed us while we munched our sandwiches with our faces to the sun. The two dogs had a rollicking good time running and exploring together. The colt and two horses, head to head, snoozed in the white sunlight, tails to the breeze. The goat jostled for a prime position under their heads where she basked in the warm steam from their noses. They obliged, quite aware that she was of course the boss. We chuckled at the smug look on her fuzzy face.

Our conversation with Jack continued where we had left off the Sunday before.

"Why do you believe in God? But more importantly, what difference does it make what we believe?" Jack forthrightly questioned. The foundation of his life philosophy was the self-sufficiency of all men to take care of themselves.

Alain, who was now deep into his French Bible, swept his arm in a wide swath across the beautiful views of the mountains in front of us. He mentioned that seeing all of this caused him to find believing in a Creator God much more plausible than the evolutionary theory that he had been taught growing up. I sat back to listen to their discussion. It had been fun watching Alain's reactions to what he had newly discovered in Scripture, reconfirming for me my own, until now, dormant beliefs.

"There were a lot of books written about the universe and how it came to be, but what strikes me is that the Bible is the only book ever written that claims to be inspired by the Creator of the universe. Not only does the inspiration for the Bible claim to be the Creator, but He is also alive. All the rest of the philosophy books I have read were written by people who are no longer living. That's impressive. I never read a book making those claims before. Everything makes more sense now," Alain added.

"But do you really think that this planet was made in six days? That sounds like such a story," Jack replied between bites of apple pie.

"I know one thing for sure, if I am going to believe in any god, He has to be so big, so mighty, so huge that He can create with just a word and a split second," Alain answered.

"Otherwise, who knows, if a man were given billions and trillions of years, he might be able to create something like that mountain or that eagle there!" I added my two cents.

Alain inserted, "Well, just knowing that there is Someone in charge of the universe brings peace to me. I grew up being fearful. And besides that, I held the belief that God was only there to punish me when I did something wrong. I am getting a completely different picture now of who He is." He tossed a pinecone at the dogs.

"As simple as that all sounds, I guess I do envy your faith," Jack concluded.

That night Alain and I began praying together, and Jack was the first person on our prayer list.

The snow was disappearing around the cabin and trees. The temperature had climbed to above freezing now during the day. So we decided to hike up as far as we could on the mountain behind us and see if we could look over the other side. It was a huge rocky mountain with a few scrubby pines, which we grabbed onto to pull ourselves up the steep slope.

We climbed ridge after ridge, gaining altitude very fast. The goat gave up after the first twenty feet, but the dog kept with us for the lower third of the climb. We sat, our feet dangling over the ridge and watched him get back to ground level and safety.

Every few minutes we stopped to rest. This was more a rock climb than a hike. At the top, we sat and ate our lunch, took some pictures, and watched the lake thaw. It was happening that fast. When we left that morning, there was only about a ten-foot patch of clear water where it melted near the mouth of the creek, but now the dark water had significantly widened. On the other side of the mountain, we looked down at the head of Chilko Lake. We could see that only the edges on that lake had frozen, and it was open in the middle.

From where we were sitting, we could not see the lodge. It was located too close to the base of the mountain. But when we stood up, we could look down the angle between our toes, and see it. A stiff breeze was blowing across the mountaintop, so we decided to take a shortcut back down through this open gorge that quickly narrowed into a shoot. We figured we could save some time by just sliding as far as we could on the smooth pebbles filling it. The trouble was, we couldn't see where it led. So Alain headed down to check it out while I anchored my heels deep into the little rocks to wait.

He was soon out of sight off to one side of the shoot. I breathed deeply to keep from panicking as I felt the marble-like rocks slowing sliding under me, pulling me toward the narrowing shoot thirty feet below me. Where was Alain? All I could hear was water faintly trickling under where I was resting. It had to be the beginnings of a creek, I mused. But this didn't relieve my anxiety. Minutes passed.

"Go back up! Don't come down any further!" I heard Alain's voice faintly calling.

"Are you OK?" I hollered.

"Yes, but it is going to be hard to get back up to where you are. Just go back up to the top and wait!"

I slowly inched my way up and onto solid ground. It was not a hard decision to wait. Rocks tumbled and slid as Alain clawed his way up. Soon he sprawled on the ground beside me.

"That shoot dropped straight off fifty feet to the rocks below," Alain breathlessly informed me.

Carefully and gratefully, we retraced our steps down the mountain where we found our dog and goat—both were happy to see us, but not nearly as happy as we were to see them!

Before we knew it summer was back, and the lodge owners flew in to prepare the resort for the season. We helped set up for the summer season for a week or two but the place was no longer ours alone and it was time to leave. We were glad to move back to the ranch. We unpacked everything at the ranch cabin, set up the animals, and then headed out to the post office and store, which was two hours away. We took our time and made a day of it.

"You're Judy of Tsuniah Lake, aren't you?" I was sitting in the truck in front of the store waiting for Alain when a man in a yellow cowboy hat walked up and stuck his head in the window.

"Yes, how did you know?"

"Oh, I listened on the radiophone all winter when you were talking to your folks!"

Not only did God know where I was but so did everyone else living out in this wilderness!

The hay season began at the ranch. Only a few weeks before, while reading his Bible, Alain had come to the conclusion that the seventh day is the Sabbath. The hay crew always took off work one day per week, Sunday, even though none of them did this for religious reasons.

"I don't understand, Alain. You told me that you believed that Jesus is the Son of God, so why would you want to have off the Jewish Sabbath?" Jack inquired.

"Well, it is actually the day commemorating the six-day creation week in the book of Genesis in the Bible," Alain smiled and answered. "There are explanations for the length of the day, the month, and the year, but I can find no logical explanation for the seven day week except the week of creation! By keeping the seventh day God set aside as a memorial, I show that I believe He is the Creator."

Jack paused, then brushed some grass off his jeans. "It's OK with me," he said. "As long as the hay doesn't lay out there on the ground." He turned quickly away, obviously moved by the reason for the request. So each Sunday during haying season, Alain raked and turned the hay alone, and it was all ready for baling every Monday morning.

The rest of the summer we spent hiking with Jack up the various surrounding mountains, and fishing in the lake. We visited with the fish camp guests and trucked over to our staked land to explore. The fine warm dry weather was a reward for tolerating June's black and deer flies.

Summer slipped quickly by, and fall was once again upon us. The aspens seemed to be holding tightly to their remaining golden leaves so that they wouldn't shiver so much in the crisp autumn breezes. The ranch cattle were gathered under the pines chewing their cud, oblivious to the changing seasons. For weeks the ducks and geese had been crossing overhead on their journey south.

"Well, this is pretty disappointing. The government declined our application for our staked land!" Alain plunked the letter down on the table, and hung his coat behind the door. "They don't give a particular reason, except to say that the area where we staked our piece has recently been removed from availability."

He had just returned from a trip to the Tatla Lake post office. The news was even cooler than the brisk breeze coming in off the lake. We sat at the table, letter in hand, contemplating our next step.

Jack was moving back closer to Williams Lake. He had been in correspondence with a widow lady he had known for years, and he was going to ask her to marry him. As much as he loved the wilderness, he didn't want to grow old out here all alone. So there would be a new manager moving in. We were welcome to stay or we could also go back to the lodge as caretakers for the winter.

There was still a month before winter would be setting in. We could go look for another piece of land to stake, but we had waited almost two years for this reply from the government, and we just wanted to have our own place somewhere.

We decided to look for a house or land to buy on Vancouver Island, and while we were down south, we would get married. My grandparents had eloped to Victoria, which is on the island, in 1909. We decided it would be a great adventure to look for the address listed on their marriage certificate and get married in the same place.

A big cathedral stood at that location with a smaller chapel attached. The pastor was in. We visited with him for awhile, and he said he would be delighted to perform our wedding ceremony. Three days later, dressed in new outfits with daisy bouquet and boutonniere, we were married in the little chapel. After a wedding dinner in a flower garden, we called our parents, who were very happy indeed to get the news.

We spent the next week looking for a place to buy, but it was expensive on Vancouver Island. Crossing over to the Olympic Peninsula in Washington state, we looked at other places, but with continued bad luck. On our last day before we had to head back north, we passed through the streets of a little Victorian village.

"A house like that would be perfect," I remarked as we drove by a little cottage. "It has a pasture with trees and even a garage. I wish it was for sale." I glanced at the front porch and there was a tiny sign that read "For Sale by Owner."

Things moved along quickly, and two months later we had moved in. Our move south was uneventful, and the animals gave us no trouble crossing the border back to the States.

We had sold our chickens to the owner of the ranch, and we gave the two rabbits to folks in Nemiah Valley who had children. Our colt,

Indigo, was sold to one of our friends on the Indian reservation. The only animals we still had were Madame, Jet, Jappeur, and Molly.

Although we loved our new place, there were few jobs available in our new town. For two months Alain did odd jobs, but he couldn't find regular work. One day when things were looking financially glum, a check arrived, totally unexpected. It was a refund check for forty-eight dollars and fifty-three cents from the Internal Revenue Service. A week before, we had received a notice from the power company that our electricity would be cut off if we were unable to pay our bill, which amounted to thirty-five dollars. We were also completely out of dog food. This check paid for both, plus the tithe on the refund!

It was now our habit to take everything to God in prayer together. That morning as we had knelt to pray to God about our situation, I had wondered if He would think it frivolous to pray for dog food when there were people in the world going without food. No one will ever convince us that the check was not an answer to prayer. It was a small thing, but it sealed our commitment to Him. And then within a month, Alain had an interesting and full-time position working for the city park service.

Part Three

Home at Last

"You shaped me before I was born;
You put my bones together while
I was still in my mother's womb . . .
How tender your thoughts have been toward me,
O Lord, how vast are their numbers!
If I wanted to count the times you have thought of me,
It would be like counting the sand on the seashore."
Psalms 139:13, 17, 18

We were driving around one afternoon in the fall when we passed a little church. I read the sign out front. "That is the same kind of church I grew up in," I mentioned as we drove by.

We had decided we didn't need to belong to an organized church. It was enough to read and study the Bible on our own and keep the seventh-day Sabbath. We even set aside tithe from Alain's paycheck.

A few weeks later I was busy painting the kitchen cupboards when I remembered an incident that happened when I was seventeen. At a church gathering our family doctor had pulled me aside and said, "I will never forget the day you were born, Judy!"

"Why, what happened?" I could not imagine what he was going to say to me.

"Your birth was a very difficult one. For hours I had attempted to turn you into a better position to be delivered but to no avail. Forceps, nothing had worked. The labor had gone on for way too long. Your mother's life was in jeopardy. It finally appeared that I would not be able to save you, so I had ordered the instruments prepared to at least save your mother's life. And then a miracle occurred, and you were born! I believe God cares a great deal for you, Judy!"

Those last words became a refrain that repeated itself with each stroke of the paintbrush. The day before I had been watching the horse and goat out the window while washing the dishes. They were a funny pair. The goat was obviously the leader because whatever direction she nibbled in, the horse was not far behind her.

A young boy pedaled by on the road. He stopped, leaned his bike against the fence, and reached over it. I couldn't hear him, but I could tell he was calling to the horse. Both animals completely ignored him. He then grabbed a handful of fescue grass from the road shoulder and tried bribing them over. It didn't work. He was a stranger to them. Defeated after several more minutes, he got on his bike and pedaled off.

Awhile later, I went out to hang up some rugs on the clothesline. Neither the goat nor the horse was in sight, so I called them. In two seconds they came trotting out of the trees at the end of the pasture and up to the fence beside me, Madame looking for all the world as if she had a happy grin on her funny face.

Of course they came to my call. They knew me and trusted me. I took care of them, cared for them. That evening long after Alain had fallen asleep, I thought about a memory verse I had learned long ago—". . . and His sheep follow Him because they know His voice . . ." (John 10:4).

How simple! I had been getting to know Jesus through talking to Him and reading His Word. I now knew how He had related to people and cared for them. This knowledge had led to my trusting Him, trusting Him with my life. I no longer just knew about Him or believed in Him. I knew Him, believed Him, trusted Him. Yes, I even loved Him because He cared for and watched out for me. This was the response, the connection, that He had been wanting from me! This had not been a burden. This was the making of a friend, the most important Friend I would ever have! What peace that gave me!

The next morning was Saturday. “What do you think about me going to that church we drove by the other day?” I said, surprising myself by verbalizing the idea to Alain. It had been ten years since I had set foot in a church.

“Well, if you would like to go, I can drop you off and pick you up,” Alain replied.

We pulled up in front of the little gray church with the steeple and sat with the motor running. The building looked benign enough, but I hesitated. “Well, maybe I will go some other time.”

“Go on ahead, you look fine,” Alain said.

“No, it’s OK. I changed my mind. Let’s go back home.”

We went back and forth like that for a few minutes. A dog barked. A slight breeze caught and tossed a red maple leaf over the truck hood. The sun came out from behind a cloud and silhouetted the church’s steeple. Suddenly, Alain got out and came around to my side. Opening the door, he leaned down. As he took my hand, he whispered, “Come, I will go with you.”

Judy & Ilana
Have van. Will travel.

Ilana & Judy in
Milan, Italy

Alain joins the
travelers

Judy and Alain in Greece

Atamamad, little friend in Kandahar, Afghanistan

Judy in Afghanistan

Mount Ararat in Turkey

Judy & Alain in Holland

Saying goodbye to the Belly Button Bomb in France

Judy & Alain hauling water at Tsuniah Lake, British Columbia, Canada

Alain skating on 12 mile long Tsuniah Lake

Molly

Jack in the Chilcotin

The de Chantal Family today ~
Jonquille & Josh
Jacinthe and Ryan with Chou Chou
Alain & Judy

More photos of this story can be found at
http://www.gypsysong.net/

One year later we were baptized and joined the Seventh-day Adventist Church. On that same day our infant daughter Jacinthe was dedicated to God. Two years later our second daughter, Jonquille, arrived, completing our family.

That day when we walked into that little church, we met the folks who would become our church family. They accepted us just as we were—my jean skirt and boots, Alain's long hair, beard and all.

As we grew into that church community, we also developed an appreciation of what it means to be a child of God. It is all about Who we know, not what we do. Oh, it is important what we do, but responding because of our love for God is what makes what we do meaningful to Him. For years I was afraid to stop and contemplate where and how I was getting through life. I was afraid of what Jesus would require of me. It was why I had slipped away, having no idea that if I had gotten to know Jesus, not just knowing about Him, I would have found what I was looking for all those years ago, that peace which passes all understanding.

It was the end of one journey—a journey of adventure and exploration—a very significant journey. But it was also the beginning of another journey, one of growing in understanding, trust, and love.

Alain and I, along with our beautiful daughters and sons-in-law, now look forward to His Second Coming with peace, knowing that He cares about even the smallest details in our lives and hears even the weakest of all prayers.

And best of all, I am most grateful that Jesus never stopped pursuing me, no matter how hard I tried to run away!

You might be wondering what happened to:

The **Belly Button Bomb** took the French kids on several trips, but on its last one, it broke down in the Saudi Arabian desert and was abandoned there in the sand.

Ilana married her childhood friend and lives in Israel. They have three grown children also living there and one grandchild. We see them whenever they come to Canada to visit her family. We went to Israel to see them, and we often talk on the phone.

Fouad, our friend in Aqaba, Jordan, lives there with several of his children nearby. We exchange letters and photos every Christmas. We visited him in 1995, the year he retired from his job at the hotel. He still had the photo we had given him when we were traveling in 1973 pinned up in his little office by the beach.

We visited Matala on Crete in 1994 and found "**Mama**" still living there. I asked her through an interpreter how she had felt about all those traveling kids living there back in the early 70s. She told us that she was grateful because she had received enough income through her little shop to send her boys to college.

Ahmed in Mashad, Iran, kept in touch with us for several years. He had his own carpet shop there and sent us the actual recipe for *abgosht*. We hope that once in awhile he remembers us as we remember him.

We do not know what happened to **Atamamad** in Kandahar, Afghanistan. We hope that he is still living after the wars. Some day it would be nice to see him again.

My **Aunt Dorothy** and **Uncle Flaten** spent their retirement years in southern Oregon until they passed away. We miss them very much but look forward to meeting them in the New Earth.

Jack got married and lived several years on a hay ranch closer to Williams Lake. He died suddenly of a heart attack about eight years after leaving the ranch. We believe that our talks about God out there in the wilderness were meaningful to him.

Frank the hippie raised goats, descendents of ours, and was living on the Chilko Lake shore in 1987 when we made a trip up there. He had more than fifty goats at that time, all of them resembling our triplets.

Once in awhile up in the Chilcotin area around Tsuniah Lake and Nemiah Valley, you will catch a glimpse of a **red-furred rabbit** or two hiding in the willow brush. Yes, our rabbits finally had children.

Judy Williams de Chantal

…was born in Seattle, Washington and grew up on Wrangell Island in Southeastern Alaska. She graduated from Auburn Adventist Academy in 1958 and Walla Walla University in 1962 with a B.S. degree in Nursing. She worked in Public Health and school nursing in Maryland and the Puget Sound area of Washington for several years.

After the events in this book, she and her husband Alain settled on the Olympic Peninsula in Washington State where they raised their two daughters on a farm full of sheep, goats, and horses, home schooling them until they entered the university.

She has always been interested in writing from an early age. Her senior year in high school she was the editor of the school paper. She went on to write humorous articles for Public Health and Tennessee Walking Horse Publications and has had a couple of stories published in Christian publications for young people.

Hiking, bike riding, reading, oil painting, knitting, and designing children's clothing are a few of her hobbies. Her oil paintings have sold through galleries and through her website (www.gypsysong.net/) to customers from Japan to Israel.

Alain and Judy's family now includes two wonderful sons-in-law. Their children live close by and they look forward to grandchildren soon.

An incidental note: Judy has Synesthesia, a 'condition' where her senses are cross-wired. In her case, words, letters, and numbers are in colors and textures which she 'feel's when she hears or says them. Singular sounds such as frogs croaking or a dial tone, are in colored, textured shapes, all 'seen' on a 'screen' about 3 or 4 feet in front of her. (Everyone has a memory 'screen' and an 'imagination 'screen' in the mind's eye. Synesthesia is just her extra 'screen'.) Any numbered system such as the centuries or shoe sizes are on what she calls 'map's and are organized in her head in colors, shapes and definite positions wrapping around her. She didn't realize until more recently, that the way she 'sees' things in her mind isn't how most other people see things.

We invite you to view the complete
selection of titles we publish at:

www.TEACHServices.com

or write or email us your praises,
reactions, or thoughts about this
or any other book we publish at:

TEACH Services, Inc.
P.O. Box 954
Ringgold, GA 30736

info@TEACHServices.com

Finally, if you are interested in seeing
your own book in print, please contact us at

publishing@teachservices.com.

We would be happy to review your manuscript for free.

www.ingramcontent.com/pod-product-compliance
Lightning Source LLC
LaVergne TN
LVHW091632100826
845152LV00001B/8

* 9 7 8 1 5 7 2 5 8 6 6 2 8 *